CHROMA

CHROMA
DESIGN ARCHITECTURE & ART IN COLOR

Barbara Glasner, Petra Schmidt (Eds.)

Birkhäuser
Basel · Boston · Berlin

CONTENTS

INTRODUCTION

CHROMA SPECTRUM 11

CHROMA CHOICE 275

APPENDIX

The Conflict of Colors
Introduction by Petra Schmidt

Mr. Pink: Why am I Mr. Pink?

Joe: Because you're a faggot, alright?

Mr. Pink: Why can't we pick our own colors?

Joe: No way. Tried it once. It doesn't work. You get four guys all fightin' over who's gonna be Mr. Black. They don't know each other, so nobody wants to back down. No way. I pick. You're Mr. Pink. Be thankful you're not Mr. Yellow.

Mr. Brown: But Mr. Brown, that's too close to Mr. Shit.

Mr. Pink: Mr. Pink sounds like Mr. Pussy. How about if I'm Mr. Purple? That sounds good to me. I'll be Mr. Purple.

Joe: You're not Mr. Purple. Some guy on some other job is Mr. Purple. You're Mr. Pink!

Mr. White: Who cares what your name is?

Mr. Pink: That's easy for you to say. You're Mr. White. You have a cool-sounding name. Alright look, if it's no big deal to be Mr. Pink, you wanna trade?

From: *Reservoir Dogs*, Quentin Tarantino, 1992

Colors as assumed names? Why not? After all, color identification has been used on the London Underground for decades. The encryption and abstraction of information using colors makes sense because they lend themselves so well to codification and orientation. This is what a previously unknown railway official called Harry Beck grasped in 1931 when he drew up a colored infographic of the London tube network, thereby providing the template for all such future diagrams. His abstract representation of the routes, stations, and transfer possibilities without regard for their physical reality, and his reduction of details to colors and lines remain exemplary even today.

But Mr. Pink doesn't want to bow to the dictates of efficiency. He rebels and initiates a conversation about the symbolism of colors. Mr. Pink, who has to consider his image as a gangster, is not at all happy with his label. Although we hardly see any colors in Quentin Tarantino's *Reservoir Dogs* because large parts of the plot are set in a white warehouse and the protagonists wear black suits and ties, the film nevertheless cleverly addresses a dilemma typically confronted when dealing with color. This dilemma is founded on a conflict with a long tradition in design and architecture between functional aspects such as signals, orientation systems, and technical implementation, and the subjective perception of color that informs the work of artists such as van Gogh, Kandinsky, and Yves Klein. In short, it concerns the opposition between emotion and rationality.

Although color, particularly in brighter variants, is commonly associated with cheerfulness and harmony, there are not many subjects that lend themselves so easily to dispute. Although centuries of cultural history have seen the attribution of powerful symbolic meanings to colors, these meanings are anything but universal. They are constantly superimposed on one another and are permeated by personal experience. In her book *Wie Farben wirken* (*How Colors Work*), sociologist and psychologist Eva Heller uses the results of an anonymous survey to show just how complex interpretations of color can be. For instance, many respondents name the color red as both the color of love and of hatred, something that does not surprise Heller since both emotions "stir up" the blood. However, she also points to other meanings attached to red. Once standing for the "privilege of the nobility," members of which had their robes dyed in the scarlet color extracted from cochineal insects, it came to be the symbolic color of communism, for in Russian the word "krasiwij" also meant "good." Thus, in Marxism-Leninism, "the reds" were synonymous with "the good," a felicitous symbol for the claim of this political grouping to be bettering the world.

Disputes about color are as old as our culture. Since Aristotle, who still assumed that the eyes emitted visual rays, science and art have been grappling with the doctrine of color. The long history of such doctrines is repeatedly marked by the publication of new insights. These have emerged in the realm of the natural sciences, as in the case of Isaac Newton's insights into refraction published in his famous work on optics (1704), from an artistic perspective, as in the case of Johannes Itten's *The Art of Color* (1961) and Josef Albers' *Interaction of Color* (1963), and in the area of technical reproduction, as seen in the *Farbenatlas* (*Color Atlas*, 1982) by researcher and printer Harald Küppers. Added to these are the numerous philosophical treatises on the subject by authors ranging from Schelling and Schopenhauer to Rudolf Steiner. "Colors lend themselves to philosophy," remarked Ludwig Wittgenstein, who for his part investigated the way language dealt with concepts of color.

And philosophy, of course, entails disputation. For instance, Johann Wolfgang Goethe's *Theory of Colours* (1840, Original: 1810) was a direct reaction to Isaac Newton's prismatic studies. Although in scientific terms the philosopher was unable to ground his theory, which was limited to the two basic colors of yellow and blue derived from "light and darkness," his theory of perception dominated philosophical debate at the time. Goethe was the first to formulate the concept that individual colors and compositions could trigger specific sensations. It was an insight that proved decisive to the emancipation of color from other elements of artistic expression such as composition and representation based on illusion. As a consequence, color was increasingly considered in isolation. Thus Wassily Kandinsky, who was influenced by Goethe's ideas, declared, "The color is the keyboard. The eye is the hammer. The soul is the piano with its many strings. The artist is the hand that purposefully sets the soul in vibrating by means of this or that key."

Goethe was thus an early exponent of the concept of color that placed the soul at its center and sparked an aesthetic debate that was to continue to exert an influence on painting as late as modernism. For example, Yves Klein saw in the production of monochromatic images an act of liberation that eliminated "psychological bars," since "before the colored surface one finds oneself directly before the matter of the soul." And the German painter Rupprecht Geiger declared, "Red makes you high." So much conviction and fervor could not but help provoke disagreement. A contrary position was soon established by painters who approached the problem of color via the intellect. The American minimalist Donald Judd, for instance, banished all psychologizing and emotional projection associated with color to the realm of obscure sciences: "[Since] the creation of science in the seventeenth century the study of color has been part of science. And like astronomy it has been cursed with its own astrology." Although artists such as Donald Judd and Gerhard Richter grappled intensively with color, they rejected a devout approach to their subject, producing pictures devoid of sentimental impetus. With his color charts, Gerhard Richter in particular concentrated on accident, indifference, and the pleasure in looking. With his color fields inspired by conventional color-sample cards he not only broke with all forms of symbolic, expressive statement but quite consciously pitted his work against the prevailing dogmas of geometric abstraction. Artists of the younger generation such as Anselm Reyle—who has gained international renown with his opulent "stripe paintings" and sculptures covered with glittering paint—and Liam Gillick—whose material collages made from plexiglass and metal clearly recall the work of Donald Judd—incorporate many of these and other historical positions in their work. Indeed, Gillick's work is characterized by the attempt on an intellectual level to mediate between design, art, architecture, and science.

However, while in art color has always been seen as an essential element and primary material of the creation of illusion in the portrayal of landscapes, spaces, and still lifes, for design it has been seen more as a quality, as an ingredient, or perhaps better put, as a "skin." This is how the Bouroullec brothers still describe color today. Their goal is to find an appropriately "natural" expression for the structures and forms they borrow from natural phenomena such as algae or clouds, including at the level of color. Their approach is thus in stark contrast to that of designers such as the Swiss Mattia Bonetti or the Spaniard Jaime Hayón, who underscore the artificial character of their creations with glittering surfaces and lush colors. They design elaborate objects as individual pieces or in limited series, which are regarded by a growing host of collectors as on a par with modern art. These designers use the same shiny and glittering surfaces that have so successfully made fetish objects out of consumer goods such as cars and cosmetics. Contemporary artists have also discovered design for themselves and the possibilities of seduction it offers. Thus, for example, Sylvie Fleury and Anselm Reyle use iridescent metallic paint for their sculptures, thus imitating the effects of the glittering everyday world.

Even in architecture a similar transformation is taking place, one that privileges the object of desire. As in the time of Bruno Taut's so-called "paintbox estates," the majority of architects still use color to emphasize facades and structural elements such as stairways, windows, and balconies, to frame them and separate them visually from the body of the building. And, as before, efficiency retains its priority, as is evident in the "machine aesthetic" about which the German designer Konstantin Grcic enthuses in his interview, which is limited to smooth, monochromatic objects and buildings, or colors that emanate from the material itself. However, recent years have seen colorful coatings being given greater consideration. Just like Grcic, who loves to render his objects monochromatic as if they had been dipped "in a bucket of paint," the Dutch architecture team MVRDV used a strictly monochromatic strategy when building their Didden Village residential complex on the roof of a former sewing workshop in Rotterdam. Without any regard for details or the structure of the building, the architects covered the simple gabled cottages and the atrium with a shiny blue layer of polyurethane, thus creating a surface that recalls colored plastic products. For the architect Louisa Hutton, who runs the Berlin firm Sauerbruch Hutton with her husband Matthias Sauerbruch, color design is also clearly a highly significant element of any architectural concept. The two architects see color as a tool and design both finely nuanced and highly colorful facades and spaces. However, this does not mean that they reject the notion of "form follows function" that had such a pronounced effect on modernism; rather, their aim is to link the position of the old masters with their own and use color as an additional "resource for creating space." As they see it, "the modernist credo of the 'truth of the material' can be extended to include the potential offered by color." This approach of the two central figures of current colored architecture is being taken much further by today's architects availing themselves of modern computer technology to design new flowing or crystalline structures. The architects associated with firms such as Massimiliano and Doriana Fuksas and UNStudio are breaking completely with the masters of modernism. In the production of their personal "machine aesthetic" they are not only using engineering programs to generate structures that recall fenders or stealth bombers. They are also transferring the colors of these objects and machines onto their structures. With the click of a mouse they color their buildings, using tones that have previously only been seen on cars and toys. The results can be seen in UNStudio's decision to bathe the auditorium of the Agora Theater in the Dutch city of Lelystad in a robust blood red, and the lush orange-red of the self-cleaning textile membrane used by Massimiliano and Doriana Fuksas to cover the Zenith concert hall in Strasbourg. Never have so many machines been seen. Even the digital glow of the computer screen can now be transferred to facades using LED technology. Now UNStudio's intricately folded facades luminesce with the gentle, colored light that we otherwise associate with the immaterial works of James Turrell. They flicker and change like a screen. Light as the source of all colors, in particular artificial and colored light, has become the central design element of an architecture that no longer aspires to be buildings but an object of desire or a usable sculpture.

In spite of all attempts here to provide a comprehensive overview of the place of color in design, art, and architecture, CHROMA is not intended as a scholarly book, an encyclopedia of color. On the contrary, it is a highly subjective response to the realization that although there is a great deal of literature on the theory of color, there are relatively few books that communicate a genuine experience of color. As the editors of this publication, this is our central concern rather than explanatory models, or color as a philosophical or scientific phenomenon, or psychology, or art history. Neither is our focus on the concrete material in terms of its materiality as seen in the works of Mark Rothko and Yves Klein, which can be explored far more effectively through the medium of an exhibition. What we are interested in is color's interplay with perception and its role as a source of inspiration. The intention of CHROMA is to stimulate, to provide an experience akin to diving into color itself, or stepping into a river dyed by Olafur Eliasson. It is about emotion rather than rationality.

CHROMA SPECTRUM

Selected by Barbara Glasner

Our everyday lives are full of color. Yet often these colors remain "invisible." They require experimentation, composition, or orchestration to come, as it were, to light. For example, when the photographer Wolfgang Tillmans captures the everyday world almost as if in passing, in an image that presents the sky and the walls of buildings or even a sheet of photographic paper as an abstract surface, tones become "visible" again. Experiencing the way color can inspire and enchant us does not necessarily mean we have to see it as a "metaphysical force" or "energy" in the way Johannes Itten did. Readers of the following chapter SPECTRUM will not need the help of metaphysics to become aware of color's riches.

Editor Barbara Glasner looked for designers, artists, and architects for SPECTRUM who approach color in a particular way and whose work—depending on the color—can be linked with monochromatic, multichromatic, or achromatic themes. The result was a very personal selection of works of great intensity in terms of color, that not only explore single colors and color combinations but also the "non-colors" black, white, and gray. Along with the great masters of color-field painting—such as Ellsworth Kelly and Imi Knoebel—SPECTRUM also features famous contemporary architects such as MVRDV and Zaha Hadid, as well as young designers such as Shay Alkalay and Maarten Baas. Rather than age, fame, or the duration of the engagement with color, it is quality and effect that have been the decisive criteria that have determined the selection presented here.

MONOCHROMATIC

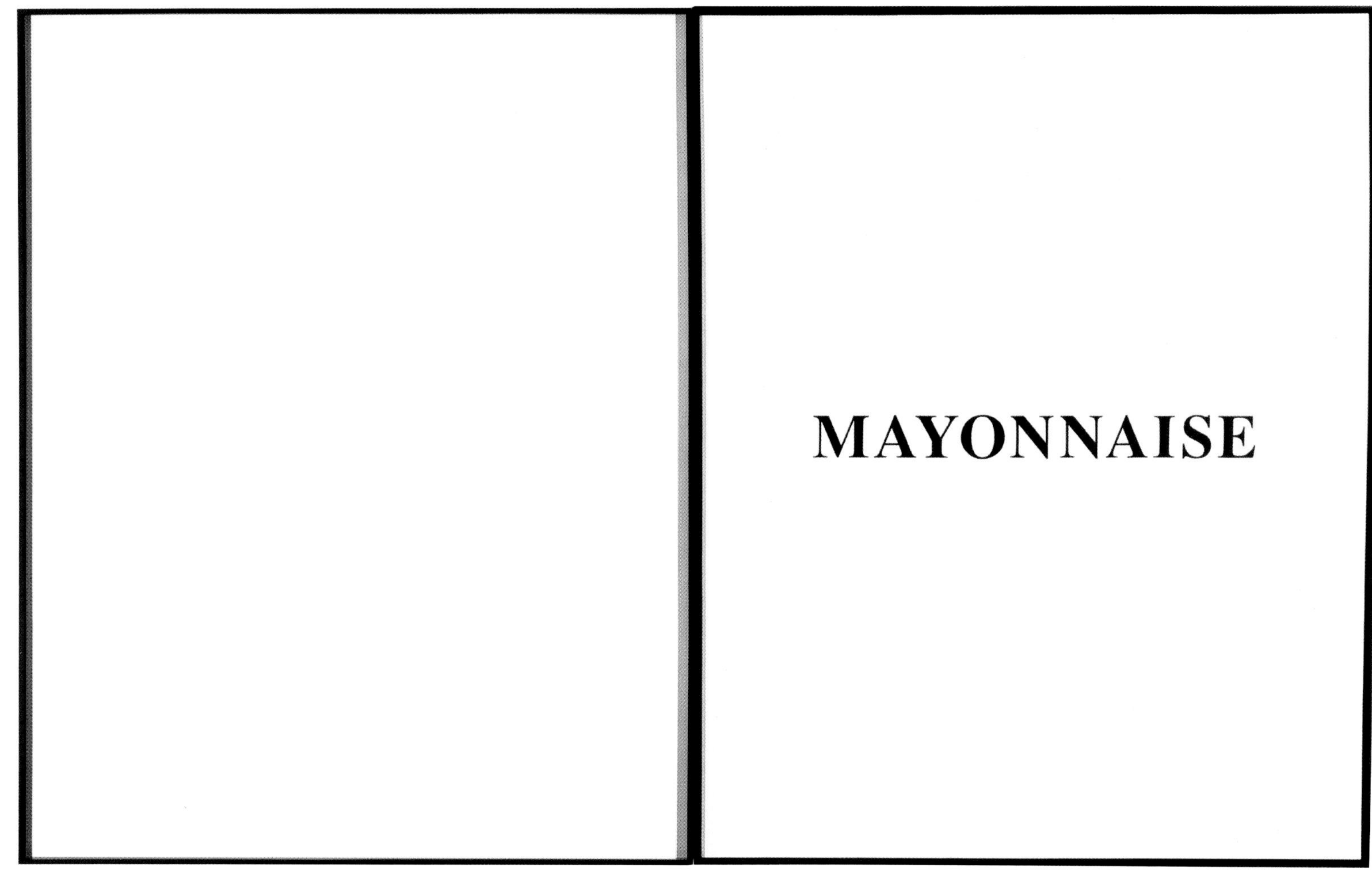

John Baldessari
Prima Facie (Fifth State): Mayonnaise, 2006
Archival Pigment Print on matt paper, acrylic on canvas
134.94 x 216.53 x 5.71 cm
Courtesy of John Baldessari, Marian Goodman Gallery, New York and Paris, and Sprüth Magers Berlin London

JÜRGEN MAYER H. Architekten
Mensa Moltke, Karlsruhe, 2007
New canteen for the Technical College, Teacher Training College and the State Academy for Fine Art
Wood structure, polyurethane finish

Amanda Levete, Future Systems
North, 2008
Console table
Fiberglass composite, fluorescent lime color
L 185 x D 70 x H 50 cm
Limited edition of 12
Manufacturer: Established & Sons

William Eggleston
Untitled, 1974

Courtesy of Cheim & Read, New York

Maarten Baas
Treasure Furniture, 2005
MDF waste from a furniture factory
H 90 x W 62 x D 55 cm

Committee, Clare Page & Harry Richardson
The Lost Twin Ornaments, 2009
Commissioned for the exhibition
“Digital Explorers: Discovery”
Courtesy of Metropolitan Works
Creative Industries Centre, London

Allford Hall Monaghan Morris Architects
Barking Central I, 2007
London Borough of Barking and Dagenham, Essex
Housing complex, aluminum facade with colored glass mosaic balconies

Berta Fischer
Phoebe, 2005
Acrylic glass
60 x 75 x 68 cm
Courtesy of Martin Asbæk Gallery, Copenhagen

SPLITTERWERK
Wohnstück (dwelling element) Übelbach, Übelbach, Austria, 1994
Facade made of yellow laminated wood panels

Maarten Van Severen
LCP (Low Chair Plastic), 2000
Acrylic glass
W 48.5 x H 70 x D 80 cm, 31 cm seat height
Manufacturer: Kartell

Ellsworth Kelly
Yellow Relief with Black, 1993
Oil on canvas, two joined panels
304.8 x 248.9 cm
San Francisco Museum of Modern Art,
gift of Doris and Donald G. Fisher

Thomas Demand
Klause V (Tavern V), 2006
C-Print/Diasec
197 x 137 cm

Courtesy of Sprüth Magers Berlin London

Studio Schellmann Furniture
Staff Lamp, 2007
Steel tube, socket
L 80, 115 or 185 cm
Courtesy of Schellmann Furniture, Munich – New York

Carsten Höller
Rhinoceros, 2005
Light yellow Biresin, blue glass eyes, horn
Approx. 120 x 80 x 50 cm
© 2009, ProLitteris, Zurich
Courtesy of Esther Schipper, Berlin and Air de Paris, Paris

Rupprecht Geiger
Gelbes Rund, 1970
Acrylic, wood
150 x 100 x 28 cm
(WV 565)

Courtesy of Geiger Archive

Katharina Fritsch
Warengestell mit Madonnen (Display Stand with Madonnas), 1987/89
Aluminum, plaster, paint
H 270, ø 82 cm

Courtesy of Matthew Marks Gallery, New York

yes architecture

Mail dispatch center, Trofaiach, Austria, 2003

Metal facade cladding in the color of the Austrian Post AG

Charlotte Posenenske
Gelbe Reliefs Serie B (Yellow Reliefs Series B), 1967
Aluminum sheet, convex folded, matt RAL yellow lacquer
100 x 50 x 14 cm
MMK Museum für Moderne Kunst Frankfurt am Main

Anish Kapoor
Yellow, 1999
Fiberglass, pigment
600 x 600 x 300 cm
Installation at Haus der Kunst, Munich, 2007
Courtesy of Lisson Gallery

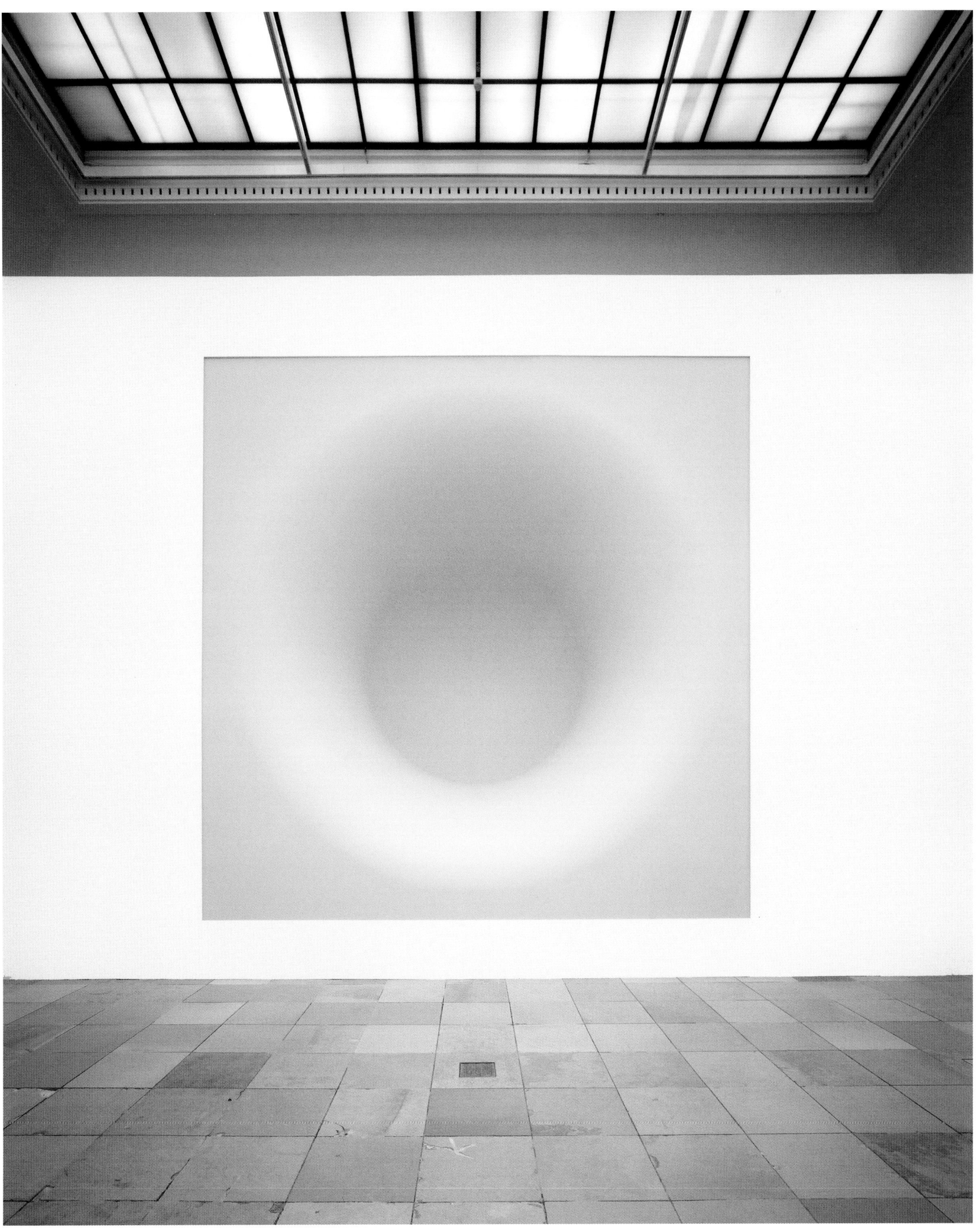

Tony Cragg
Outspan, 2007
Bronze
95 x 100 x 62 cm

Joachim Grommek
B9, 2007
Lacquer, acrylic, oil, primer
on laminated chipboard
65 x 50 cm
Courtesy of VOUS ETES ICI, Amsterdam

Rojkind Arquitectos
Nestlé Application Group, Querétaro, Mexico, 2009
Laboratory and office building

Olafur Eliasson
***The yellow colour circle*, 2008**
From *The colour circle series*, part 2
Color gravure
171 x 175 cm
Courtesy of Olafur Eliasson; neugerriemschneider, Berlin;
Niels Borch Jensen Galerie und Verlag, Berlin;
Tanya Bonakdar Gallery, New York

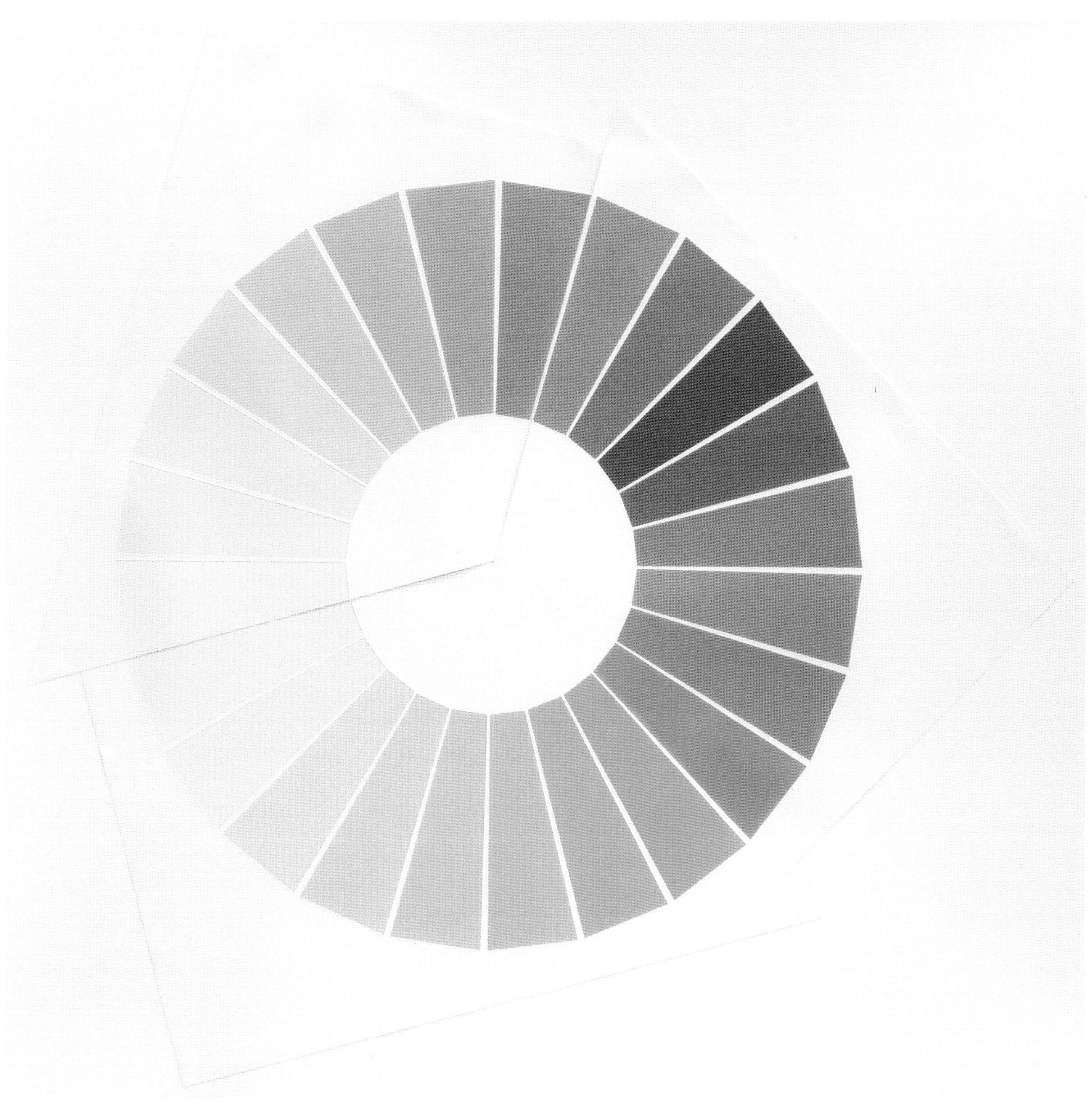

Saskia Diez
Gold Sapphire Bracelet from the "Diamonds" series
Solid gold-plated bronze in sapphire cut, elastic thread
1.8 x 1.8 cm (per stone)

BLESS
Golden Pearls (Collection BLESS N°26 Cable Jewellery)
Electricity cable, plastic beads
Courtesy of BLESS

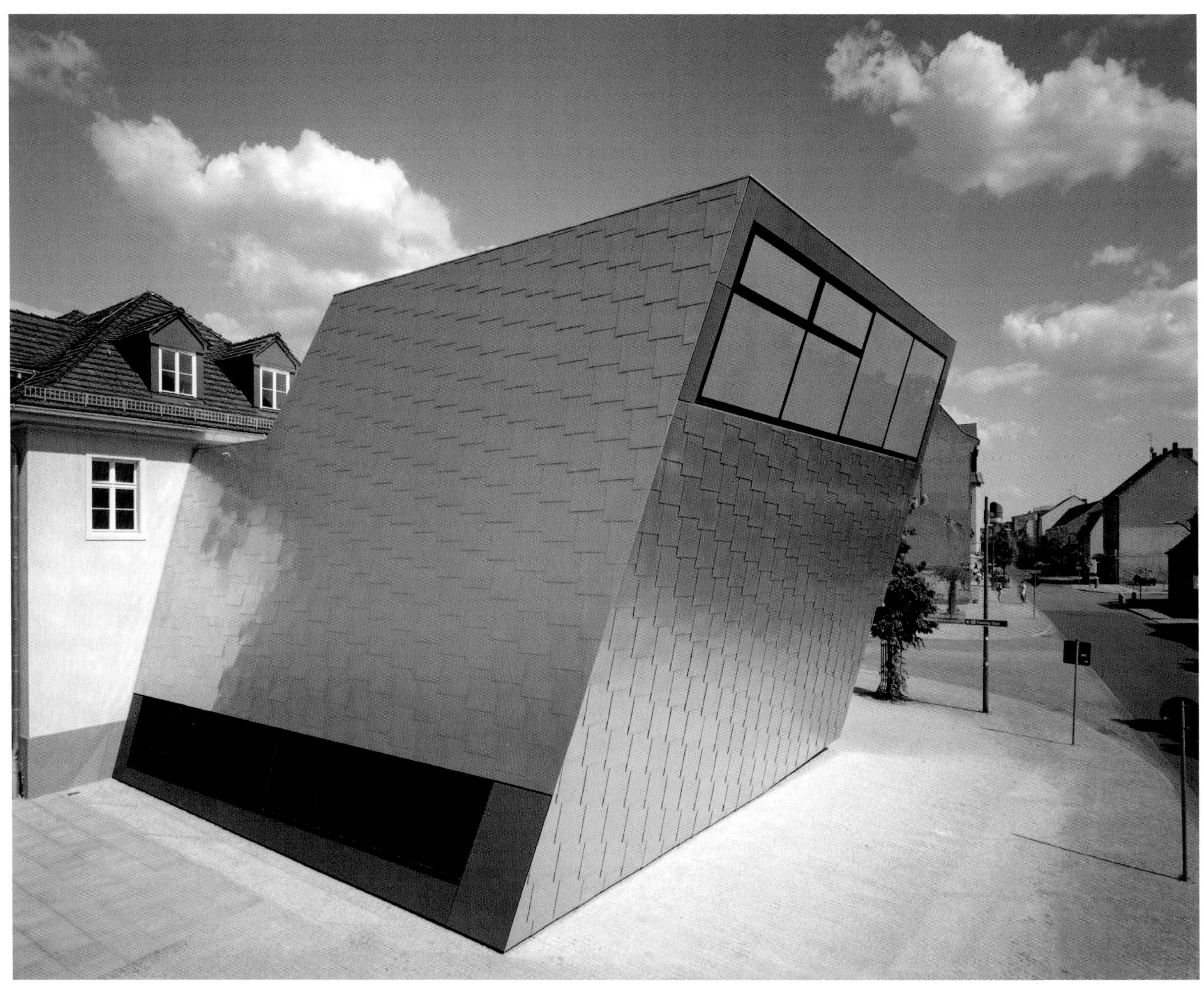

ff-Architekten & Martina Wronna
Library at Luckenwalde station, Luckenwalde, Germany, 2008
Conversion of an old railway station and annexe building

Studio Job
Bottle Rack, Farm, 2008
Polished bronze, glass
Edition of 6 + 2 A.P.
30 x 15 x 35 cm
Collection eg. Zuiderzee Museum

Mattia Bonetti
Toast, 2007
Side table made of fiberglass, metallic paint
H 60 x W 67 x D 57 cm
Editions David Gill, limited to 8 + 2 P. + 2 A.P.

Courtesy of David Gill Galleries

William Eggleston
Untitled, from "Graceland," 1983

Courtesy of Cheim & Read, New York

Tham & Videgård Hansson Arkitekter
Refurbishment of an apartment at Humlegården, Stockholm, 2008
Multi-colored parquet on floors and walls

Sylvie Fleury
Mushroom (BC 08 Gemini 0006), 2007
Fiberglass, metallic car paint
H 110, ø 80 cm
Courtesy of Galerie Thaddaeus Ropac Salzburg – Paris

Joachim Grommek
B2, 2007
Lacquer, acrylic, oil, primer
on laminated chipboard
65 x 50 cm
Collection Werner Driller, Bochum
Courtesy of VOUS ETES ICI, Amsterdam

MVRDV
Studio Thonik, Amsterdam, 2001
Originally painted in orange. Following complaints
from the neighbors, repainted in green.
Image: original color

Katharina Grosse
Untitled, 2008
Acrylic on diverse material
750 x 1200 x 500 cm
Installation view: New Orleans Biennial

Richard Woods
Wrongwoods, 2007
Woodblock print pattern
Chest of drawers designed by Sebastian Wrong
L 109.2 x W 50.8 x H 73.6 cm
Manufacturer: Established & Sons

Raw-Edges, Shay Alkalay
Stack, 2008
H 180 cm
Chest of drawers with flexible elements
Manufacturer: Established & Sons

Shaan Syed
Shoegazer Number Four, 2008
Oil and polyfilla on canvas
183 x 153 cm
Courtesy of Galerie Michael Janssen, Berlin
© Shaan Syed

Anish Kapoor
7 Ways In, 2000
Stainless steel, lacquer
152.6 x 104 x 97.2 cm
Courtesy of Regen Projects

dRMM (de Rijke Marsh Morgan Architects)
Wansey Street Housing, Elephant & Castle, London, 2006
Timber-backed facade panels of fiber cement

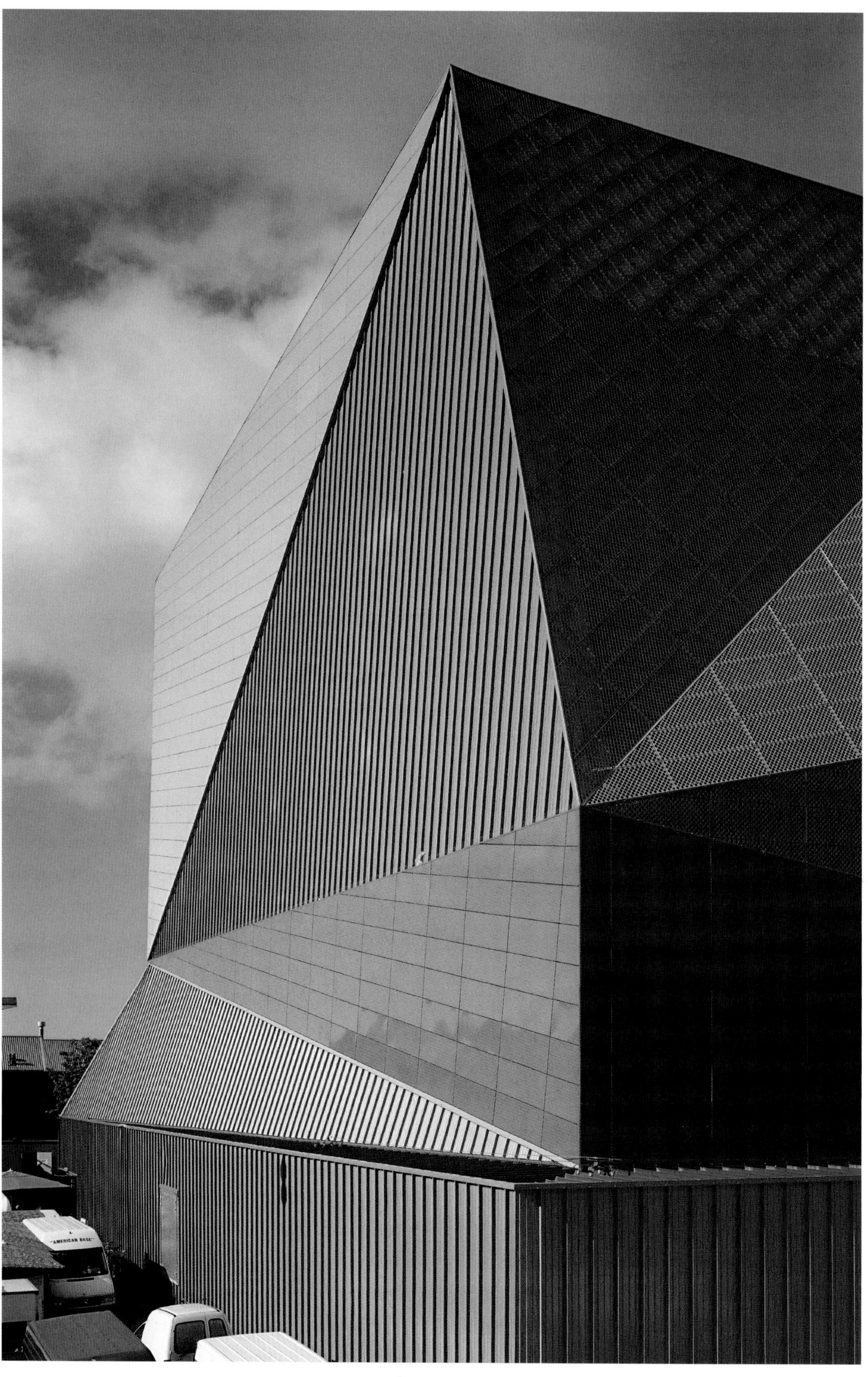
"AMERICAN BASE"

UNStudio
Agora Theater, Lelystad, The Netherlands, 2007
Multi-faceted perforated surface
with a kaleidoscopic effect

Imi Knoebel
Mennigebild 3/20, 1976/2007
Acrylic, wood
214 x 360 x 8.7 cm
2008 Collection Valticos, Geneva

Massimiliano & Doriana Fuksas
Zenith Music Hall, Strasbourg, 2007
Metal facade structure,
orange translucent textile membrane

Carsten Höller
Upside-Down Mushroom Room, 2000
480 x 1230 x 730 cm
© 2009, ProLitteris, Zurich
Courtesy of Fondazione Prada, Milan

Ellsworth Kelly
Red-Orange Panel with Curve, 1993
New York, Museum of Mordern Art (MoMA)
Oil on canvas
269.4 x 222.5 cm
Gift of the Committee on Painting and Sculpture
in honor of Richard E. Oldenburg
©2009. Digital image, The Museum of Modern Art,
New York/Scala, Florence

Stefan Diez
CH04 Houdini, 2009
Oak-veneered plywood, lacquer
L 50 x W 57.5 x H 80 cm
Manufacturer: e15

Richard Woods
RENOVATION, 48 Merton Hall Road, 2005
Wimbledon, London
Courtesy of Artworks in Wimbledon

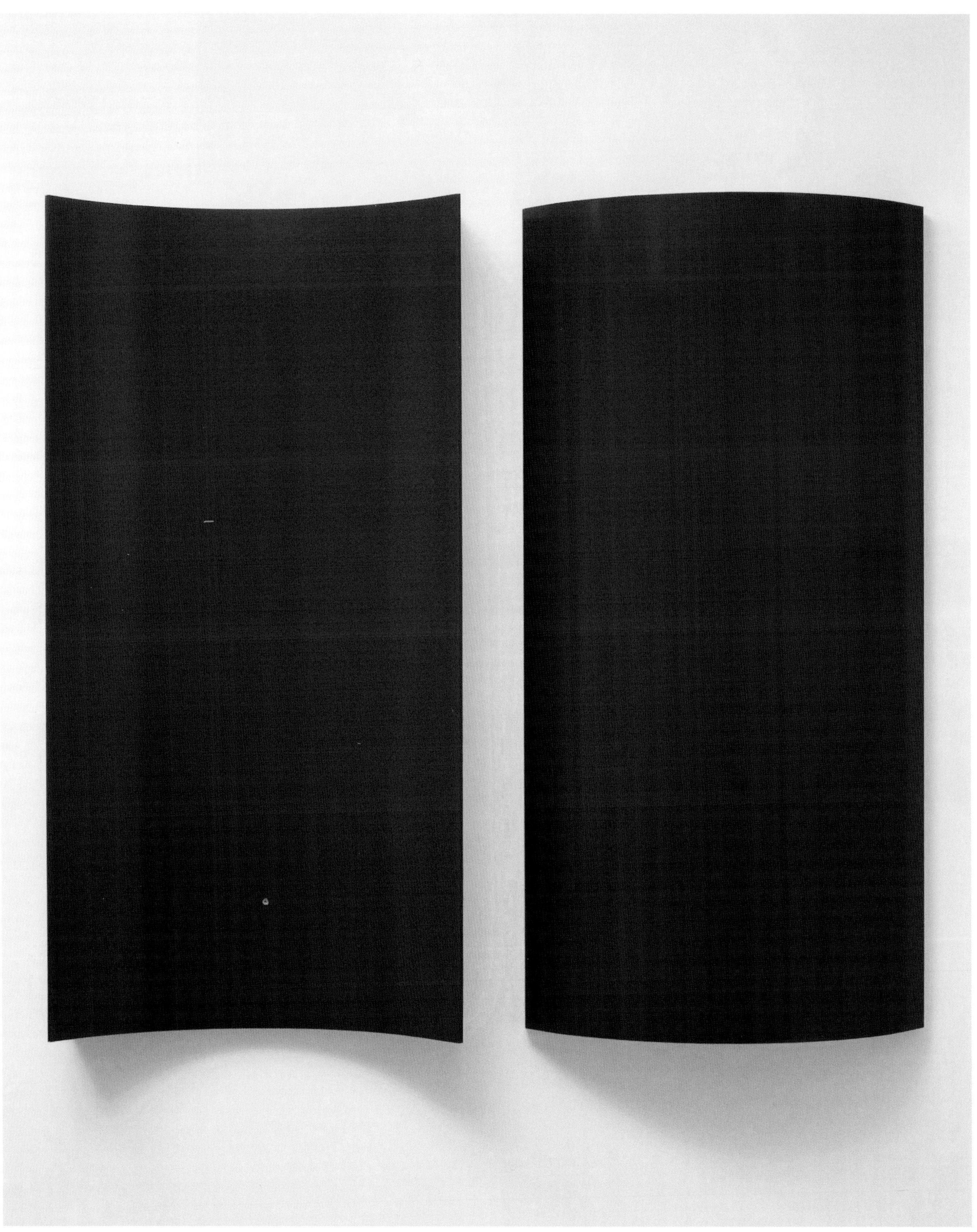

Charlotte Posenenske
Rote Reliefs Serie B (Red Reliefs Series B), 1967
Aluminum sheet, convex and concave curved,
matt RAL red lacquer
100 x 50 x 14 cm
Artist's estate

Pierre Charpin
large r, 2005
Coffee table from "The Platform Collection"
Brushed and lacquered aluminum
Max. L 160 x max. W 87 x H 35 cm
Limited edition of 8 + 2 A.P. + 2 prototypes
Manufacturer: Galerie Kreo

John Baldessari
Person with Guitar (Red), 2005
Five-color screenprint mounted on Sintra
76.2 x 92.08 cm
Courtesy of John Baldessari, Marian Goodman Gallery, New York and Paris, and Sprüth Magers Berlin London

James Turrell
A Frontal Passage, 1994
New York, Museum of Modern Art (MoMA)
Fluorescent light installation, dimensions variable
Museum installation: 391.2 x 685.8 x 1036.3 cm
Douglas S. Cramer, David Geffen, Robert and Meryl Meltzer, Michael and Judy Ovitz
© 2009. Digital image, The Museum of Modern Art, New York/Scala, Florence

Maison Martin Margiela
Garment from the MMM 20th anniversary show
Spring/summer 2009
Runway image

Ronan & Erwan Bouroullec
Galerie Kreo exhibition, 2008
Paravent
Metal structure, foam, and textile
200 x 260 x 44 cm

Rojkind Arquitectos
Casa pR34, Tecamachalco, Mexico, 2003

Steel-plate facade, car paint

Zaha Hadid
Red Aqua Table, 2005
Polyurethane, gloss finish
L 305 x W 132 x H 76 cm
Limited edition of 39
Manufacturer: Established & Sons

UNStudio
Agora Theater, Lelystad, The Netherlands, 2007
Interior view

Tony Cragg
Red Square, 2007
Bronze
116 x 73 x 70 cm
Courtesy of Marian Goodman Gallery, New York

Rojkind Arquitectos
Nestlé Chocolate Museum, Mexico City, 2007
Entrance hall with reception, auditorium, and museum shop

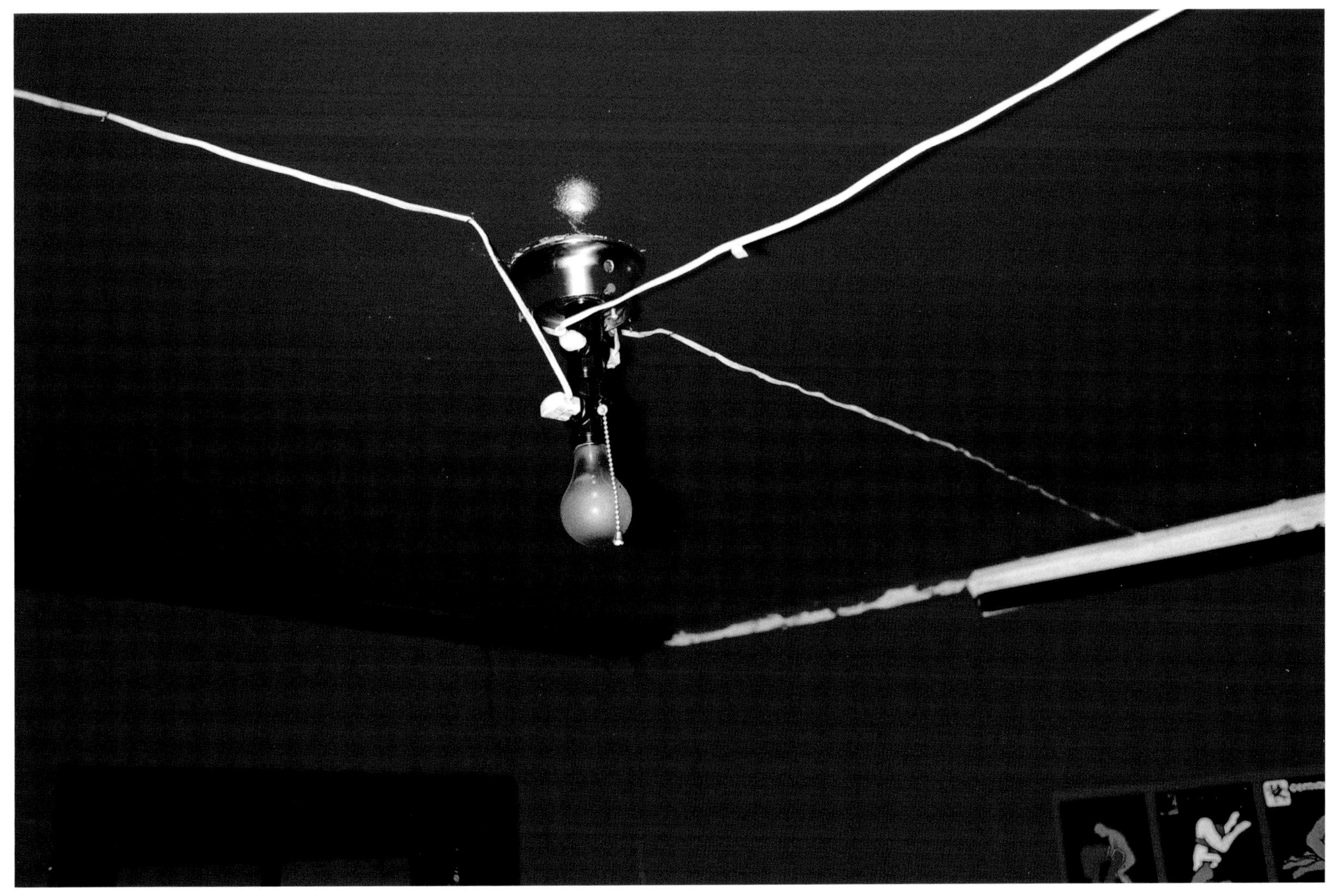

Katharina Fritsch
Händler (Dealer), 2001
Polyester, paint
192 x 59 x 41 cm
© Katharina Fritsch/2009, ProLitteris, Zurich
Courtesy of Matthew Marks Gallery, New York

William Eggleston
Greenwood, Mississippi, 1973
© Eggleston Artistic Trust
Courtesy of Cheim & Read, New York

Maison Martin Margiela
Pearly Dress (Women)
Artisanal collection spring/summer 2008
Silk chiffon with embroidered vintage buttons

Anish Kapoor
Svayambh, 2007
Wax, oil-based paint
Dimensions variable
Installation view: Musée des Beaux-Arts de Nantes

Liam Gillick
LAPSED REDUCTION, 2008
Powder-coated aluminum, transparent red acrylic glass
W 300 x D 30 x H 200 cm
Unique
Courtesy of Liam Gillick and Casey Kaplan, New York

Wolfgang Tillmans
paper drop (red), 2006
C-Print, various sizes
Courtesy of Galerie Daniel Buchholz, Cologne

Eva Marguerre
Nido, 2008
Stool series, fiberglass, 4 variations
Each approx. L 30 x W 30 x H 45 cm, each approx. 900 gr
Manufacturer: Masson

BarberOsgerby
Iris 600, 2008
Anodised aluminum, glass
H 63, ø 50 cm
Limited edition of 12
Manufacturer: Established & Sons

Wolfgang Tillmans
Lighter 69, 2006
C-Print in acrylic glass frame
65 x 54 x 12.5 cm
Courtesy of Galerie Daniel Buchholz, Cologne

Andreas Exner
Rote Hose (Red Trousers), 1993
Fabric, sewed
Approx. 103 x 41 cm

Courtesy of Galerie Horst Schuler, Düsseldorf

Ronan & Erwan Bouroullec
Clouds, 2008
Textile modules, thermo-compressed foam and fabric, rubber bands
Manufacturer: Kvadrat

Jaime Hayón
Blackberry Freeze from "The Crystal Candy Set," 2009
Crystal
L 22 x H 38.3 cm
Numbered and limited edition of 25
Manufacturer: Baccarat

Rupprecht Geiger
Rollenbild (Pinc vital), 1991
Acrylic, canvas
203 x 137.5 x 8.5 cm
(WV 813)
Privately owned, Germany

Courtesy of Geiger Archive

Verner Panton
Multi-functional living unit, 1966
Chrome-plated steel frame, wood and foam upholstery,
red nylon velours
250 x 198 x 198 cm
Prototype
Manufacturer: Behr Möbel in cooperation with DUX-Möbel

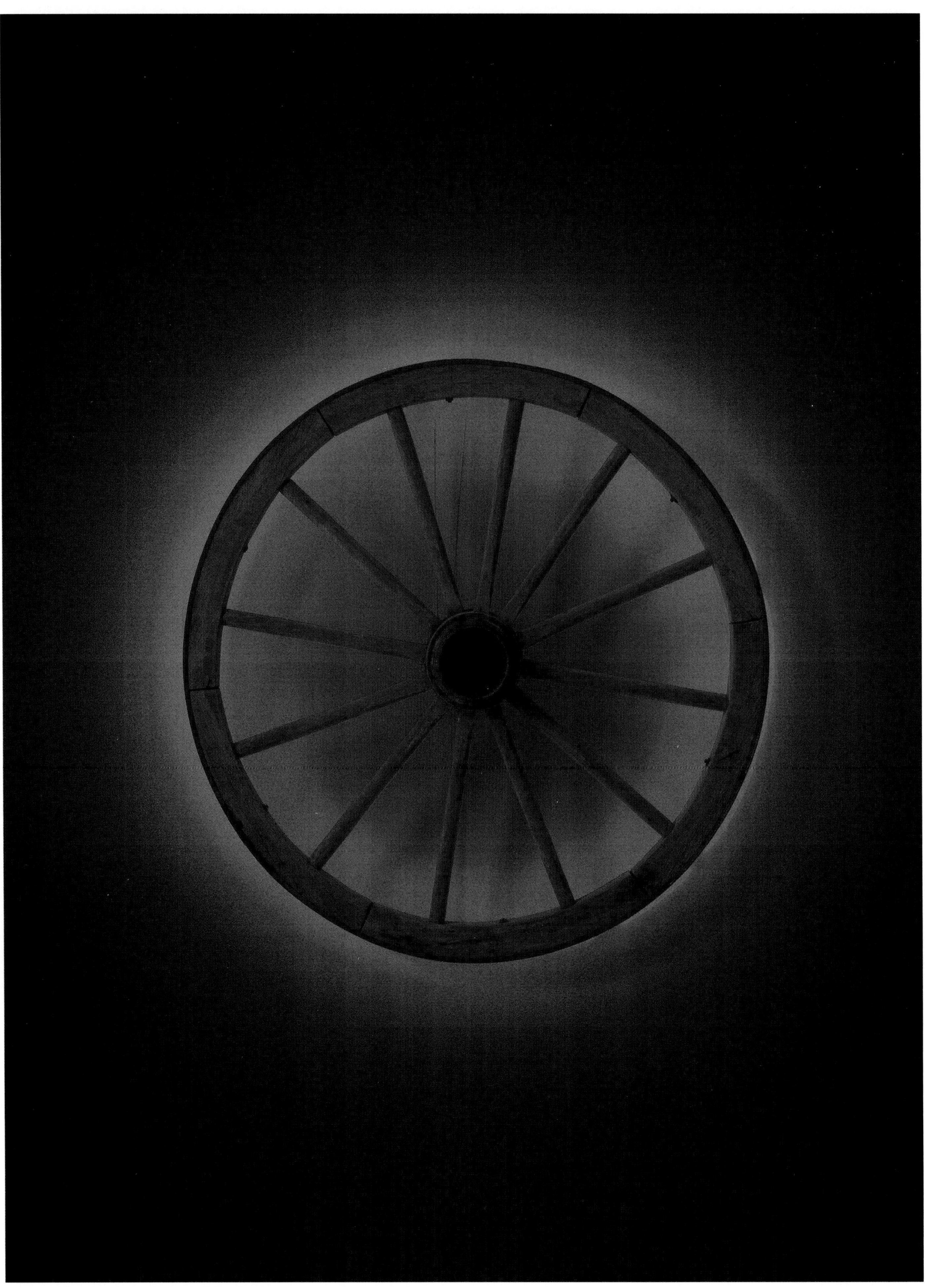

Anselm Reyle
Wagon wheel, 2007
Found object, neon tube
ø 110 cm
Private collection

Courtesy of Gagosian Gallery, New York

Maison Martin Margiela
Leather boot
MMM collection, autumn/winter 2007/2008

Tham & Videgård Hansson Arkitekter
Refurbishment of an apartment at Humlegården, Stockholm, 2008
Multi-colored parquet on floors and walls

Saskia Diez
Pink Red Wood Necklace from the "Wood" series
Beechwood, polished, glazed, lacquered
L 100 cm, ø wood bead 0.1 cm

Nitzan Cohen
nan15, bookshelf, 2008
Sheet steel 0.2 cm, powder-coated
Each W 46.8 x D 31.4 x H 19.2 cm
Manufacturer: nanoo by Faserplast

Yves Klein
Monochrome rose sans titre (MP 30), 1955
100.3 x 64.4 cm

Courtesy of Yves Klein Archives, Paris

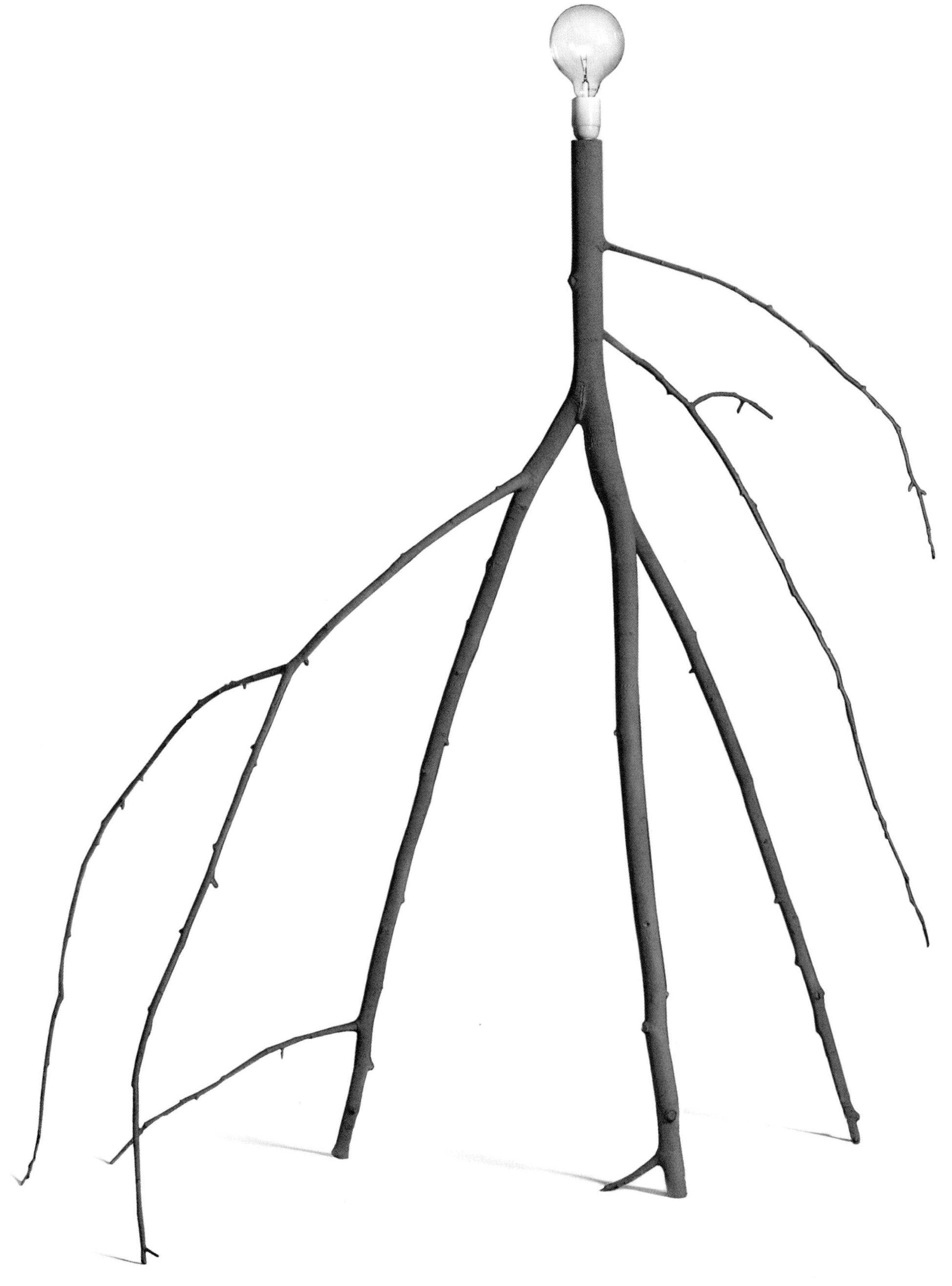

Front
Treelamp, 2006
Part of the project "Bar by Front," Stockholm
Natural branches, variable dimensions

Carsten Höller
Hippopotamus, 2007
Pink Biresin, horn, blue glass eyes
Approx. 90 x 55 x 30 cm
Private collection, Monaco

Courtesy of Air de Paris, Paris

Joachim Grommek
B12, 2007
Lacquer, acrylic, oil, primer
on laminated chipboard
65 x 50 cm
Courtesy of VOUS ETES ICI, Amsterdam

Pierre Charpin
Parabole, 2008
Free standing lamp, wall mounted lampshade
Lamp: 185 cm, lampshade: D 37.8, ø 130 cm
Limited edition of 8 + 2 A. P. + 2 prototypes
Manufacturer: Galerie Kreo
Courtesy of Galerie Kreo, Paris

Hella Jongerius
Artificial vase Rose "#2," Collection "Natura Design Magistra," 2009
Vase: pink glass, terracotta, tape
Flower: blown glass
H 117 cm (total dimension)
Numbered unique piece
Courtesy of Galerie Kreo, Paris

ahrens grabenhorst architekten
Kunstmuseum Celle with Robert Simon Collection, Celle, Germany, 2006
Conversion and annexe building

Tom Dixon
Pipe, 2006
Extruded aluminum, powder-coated and anodised
H 65, ø 15 cm
Manufacturer: Tom Dixon

Mattia Bonetti
Pearl, 2007
Table made of fiberglass, metallic paint
H 45 x W 150 x D 100 cm
Editions David Gill, limited to 8 + 2 P. + 2 A.P.

Courtesy of David Gill Galleries

Andreas Exner
Lila Hose (Purple Trousers), 2003
Fabric, sewed
Approx. 110 x 63 cm
Mondstudio Collection

Courtesy of Galerie Horst Schuler, Düsseldorf

Herzog & de Meuron
Forum, Barcelona, 2004
Facade made of colored shotcrete

John Baldessari
Prima Facie (Fifth State): Creative Thinker, 2007
Archival print mounted on aluminum, acrylic on canvas
135.89 x 218.44 x 5.71 cm
Courtesy of John Baldessari, Marian Goodman Gallery, New York and Paris, and Sprüth Magers Berlin London

Sylvie Fleury
Mushroom (KK 700 True Blasberry), 2005
Fiberglass, metallic car paint
H 110, ø 80 cm
Courtesy of Galerie Thaddaeus Ropac Salzburg – Paris

Ron Arad
Misfits, 2007
Steel frame, foam
Manufacturer: Moroso

Shaan Syed
Shoegazer Number Ten, 2009
Oil and polyfilla on canvas
183 x 153 cm
Courtesy of Galerie Michael Janssen, Berlin

Lederer + Ragnarsdóttir + Oei
Gustav-von-Schmoller school, Heilbronn, 2003
Extension to a school complex

Scholten & Baijings
Colour Plaid 01, 2005
Merino wool and cotton
140 x 180 cm and 280 x 260 cm
Manufacturer: Scholten & Baijings and De Ploeg

Tony Cragg
McCormack, 2007
Bronze
117 x 130 x 75 cm
Courtesy of Thaddaeus Ropac Gallery, Salzburg – Paris

Peter Zimmermann
Untitled, 2008
60 x 45 cm
Epoxy on canvas

Courtesy of Galerie Michael Janssen, Berlin

Jaime Hayón
Funghi, 2006
Porcelain lamps
ø 16 to 38 cm, H 36 to 50 cm
Manufacturer: Metalarte

von Gerkan, Marg und Partner (gmp)
High Tech Park, Heavy Industry Zone, Lingang New City, China, 2007
Facade

Jean Nouvel
Concert hall, Copenhagen, 2009
Blue fiberglass facade

Yves Klein
Sculpture éponge sans titre (SE 33), 1961
Pure pigment and resin, natural sponge
42 x 37 x 20 cm

Courtesy of Yves Klein Archives, Paris

Maarten Baas
Clay Furniture, Floor Fan, 2006
Metal frame, hand-modeled industrial plasticine, lacquer
H 152.4 x W 48.3 x D 48.3 cm
Manufacturer: Maarten Baas

Baumschlager Eberle
Nordwesthaus, Fussach, Austria, 2008
Concrete structure with glass facade

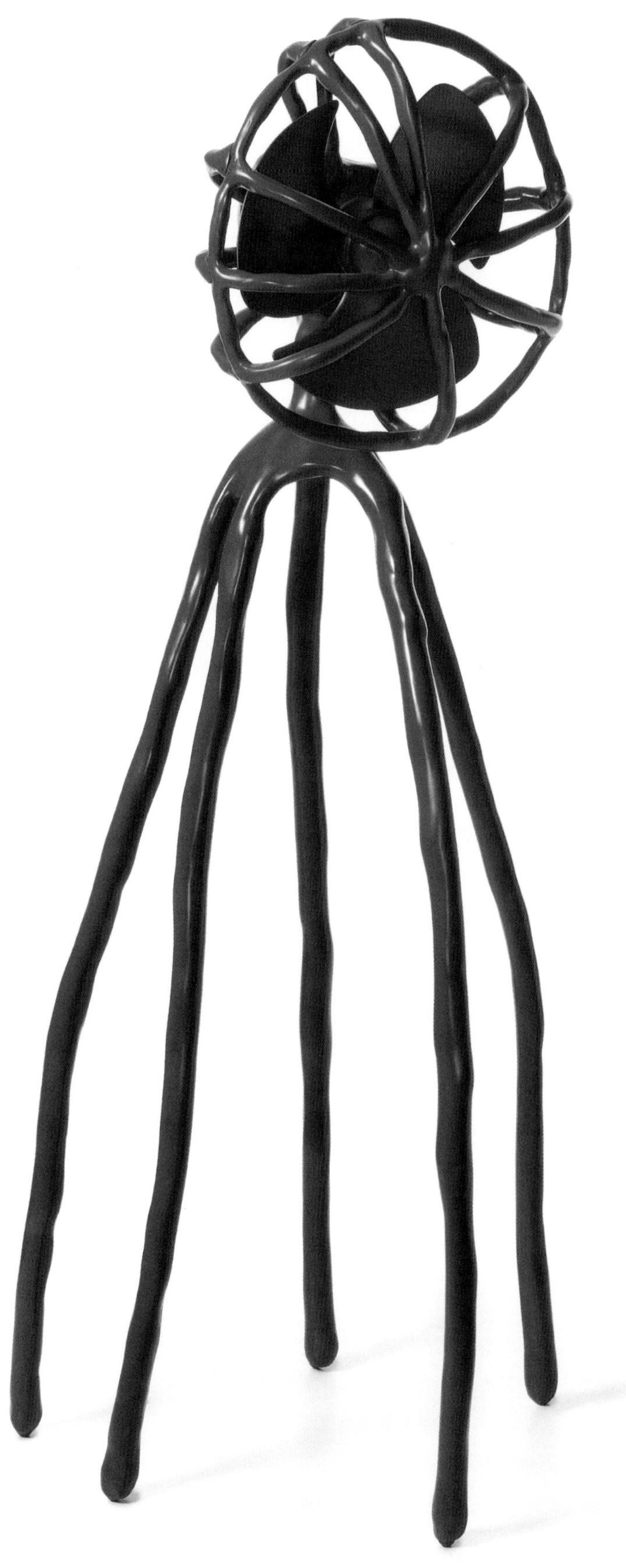

Arik Levy
Rock Fusion Soft, 2008
Polyethylene structure with fabric upholstery
Limited edition
Manufacturer: Ldesign

Charlotte Posenenske
Faltung (Fold), 1965
Aluminum sheet, RAL blue lacquer
86 x 100.5 x 14.5 cm
Signed and dated: CP 65, Collection of Sandra Kranich
and Jochem Hendricks, Frankfurt am Main

Rupprecht Geiger
Color design for Joseph-von-Fraunhofer school, Munich, 1973
III. Semi-circle, swimming pool
Acrylic, fiber-cement slabs
388 x 1035 cm
© 2009, ProLitteris, Zurich
Courtesy of Geiger Archive

Wolfgang Tillmans
Lighter II, 2006
C-Print in acrylic glass frame
65 x 54 x 12.5 cm
Courtesy of Galerie Daniel Buchholz, Cologne

REVIVE

Sylvie Fleury
Revive, 2001/02
Blue neon light
80 x 360 cm
Courtesy of Galerie Thaddaeus Ropac Salzburg – Paris

Fernando & Humberto Campana
Aster Papposus, 2006
Seating element, two volumes in expanded polyurethane
Manufacturer: edra

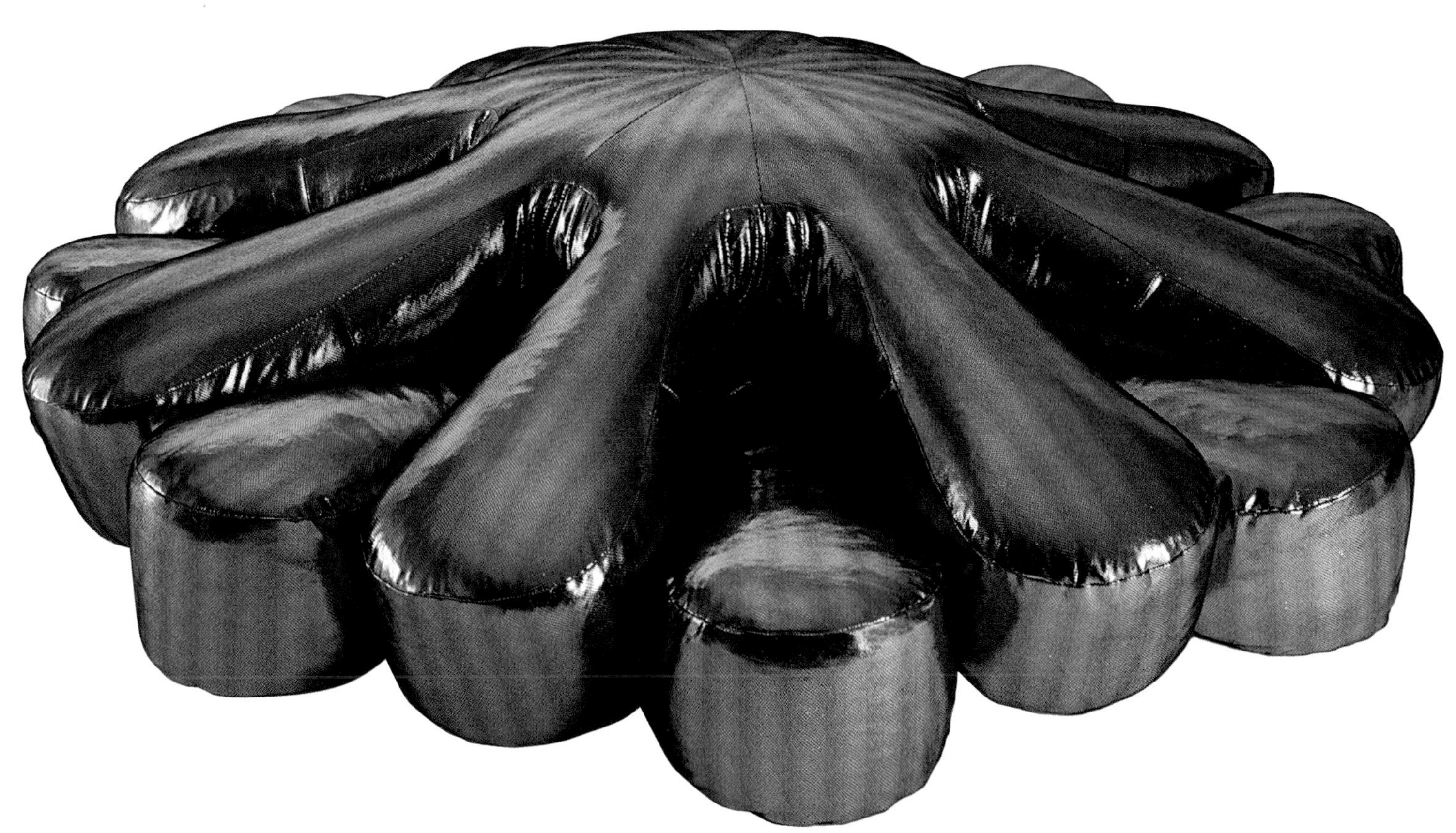

BarberOsgerby
Aluminum Shell Chair, 2007
Polished aluminum, lacquer
Edition of 8 for 20ltd

Dan Flavin
Untitled, 1997
Permanent exhibition site at the church of
Santa Maria in Chiesa Rossa, Milan
Fluorescent light in blue, red, yellow, and ultraviolet

Courtesy of Fondazione Prada, Milan

MVRDV
Didden Village, Rotterdam, 2007
Extension to a private residence
Blue polyurethane coating
Aerial photo and view of roof terrace

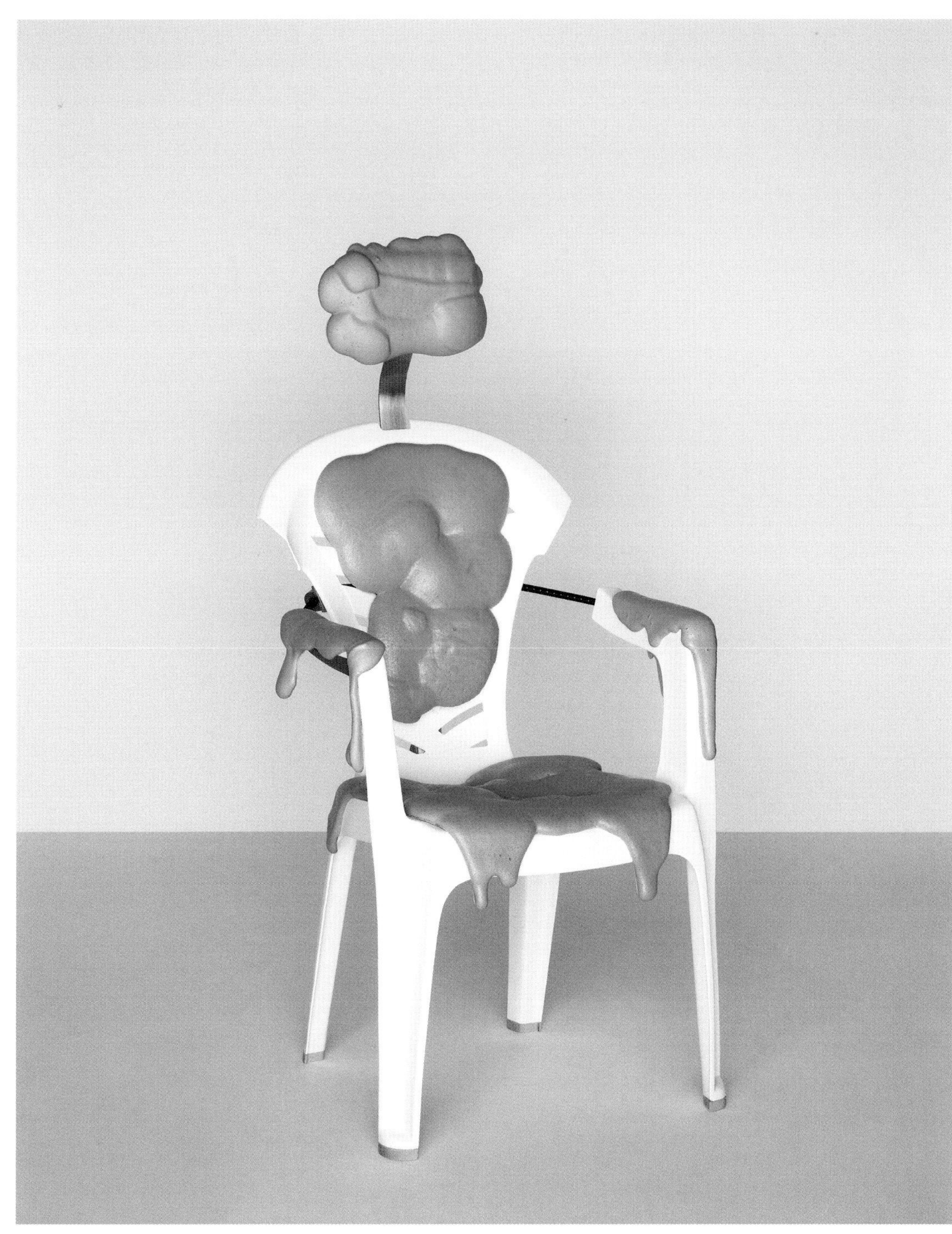

Wolfgang Tillmans
himmelblau, 2005
C-Print, various sizes
Courtesy of Galerie Daniel Buchholz, Cologne

Jerszy Seymour
New Order, 2007
Polypropylene, metal, polyurethane
L 115 x W 54 x H 54 cm
Prototype for Vitra Edition
Manufacturer: Vitra

Keisuke Fujiwara
Spool Chair (Fire/Water), 2008
"Thonet No. 14" chair,
wrapped with 6 km of thread

BarberOsgerby
Iris 1300, 2008
Anodised aluminum, glass
H 40, ø 130 cm
Limited edition of 12
Manufacturer: Established & Sons

Pierre Charpin
Cargo, 2008
Matt varnished aluminum
L 190 x W 70 x H 30 cm
Limited edition of 8 + 2 A. P. + 2 prototypes
Manufacturer: Galerie Kreo
Courtesy of Galerie Kreo, Paris

Maarten Van Severen
Kast met gekleurde deuren, 2000
Cupboard with sliding doors,
5 different types of aluminum surfaces
W 357.7 x H 144.8 x D 40 cm
Edition for Galerie Kreo, Paris
Manufacturer: tm, division topmouton

Ayzit Bostan
Ayzit 1, 2008
Leather bag
Manufacturer: Bree

SPLITTERWERK
Grüner Laubfrosch (Green Tree Frog), St. Josef, Austria, 2004
Green translucent corrugated polyester boards
with neon tubes

BarberOsgerby
Lanterne Marine, 2009
Hand blown glass, anodised aluminum frame
Limited edition
Manufacturer: Venini

Tony Cragg
On a Roll, 2003
Bronze
82 x 95 x 95 cm

Pierre Charpin
medium t, 2005
Coffee table from "The Platform Collection"
Brushed and lacquered aluminum
Max. L 140 x max. W 81 x H 35 cm
Limited edition of 8 + 2 A.P. + 2 prototypes
Manufacturer: Galerie Kreo

Maarten De Ceulaer
A Pile of Suitcases, 2008
Multiplex, hardboard, various types of leather
L 115 x W 65 x H 210 cm
Limited edition of 12 + 3 A.P. for Nilufar gallery, Milan

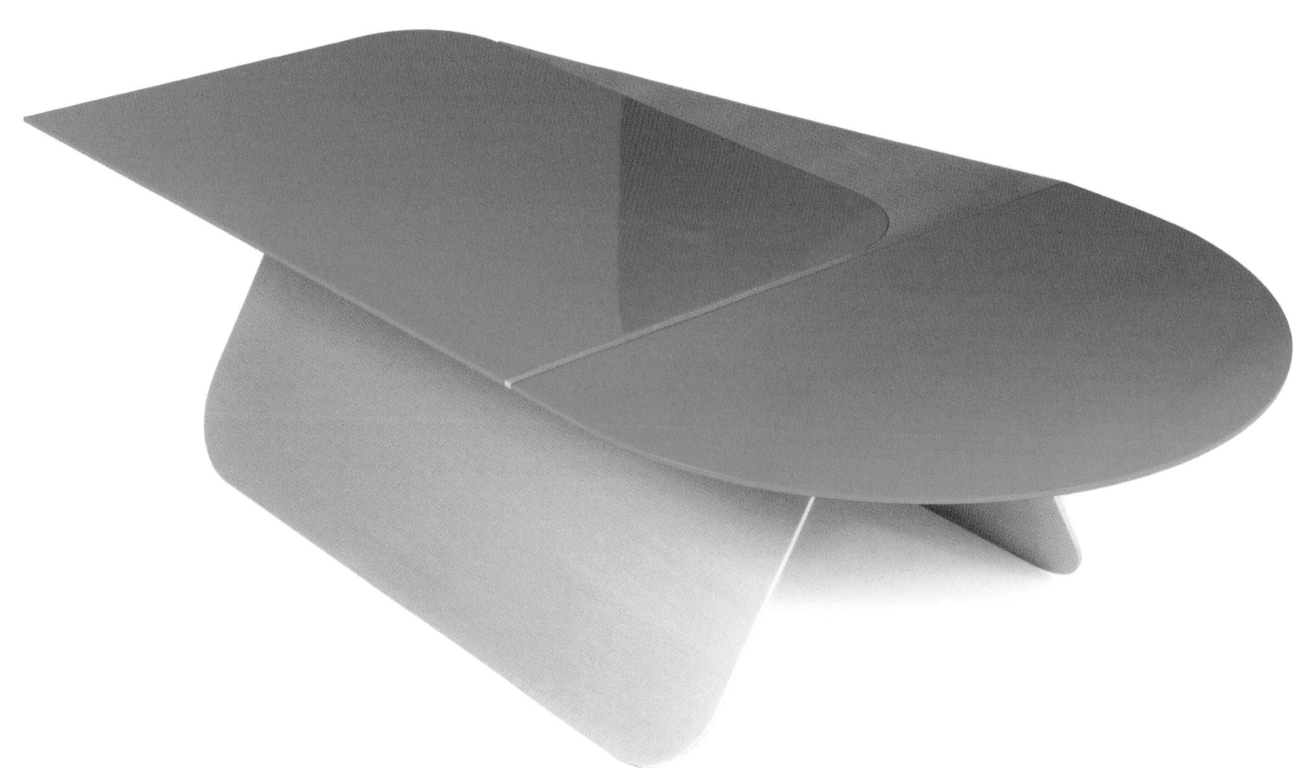

Andreas Exner
Grüner Rock (Green Skirt), 1992
Fabric, sewed
Approx. 60 x 64 cm
Kienbaum Collection

Courtesy of Galerie Horst Schuler, Düsseldorf

Berta Fischer
Yola, 2007
Acrylic glass
110 x 147 x 125 cm
Courtesy of Galerie Giti Nourbakhsch, Berlin

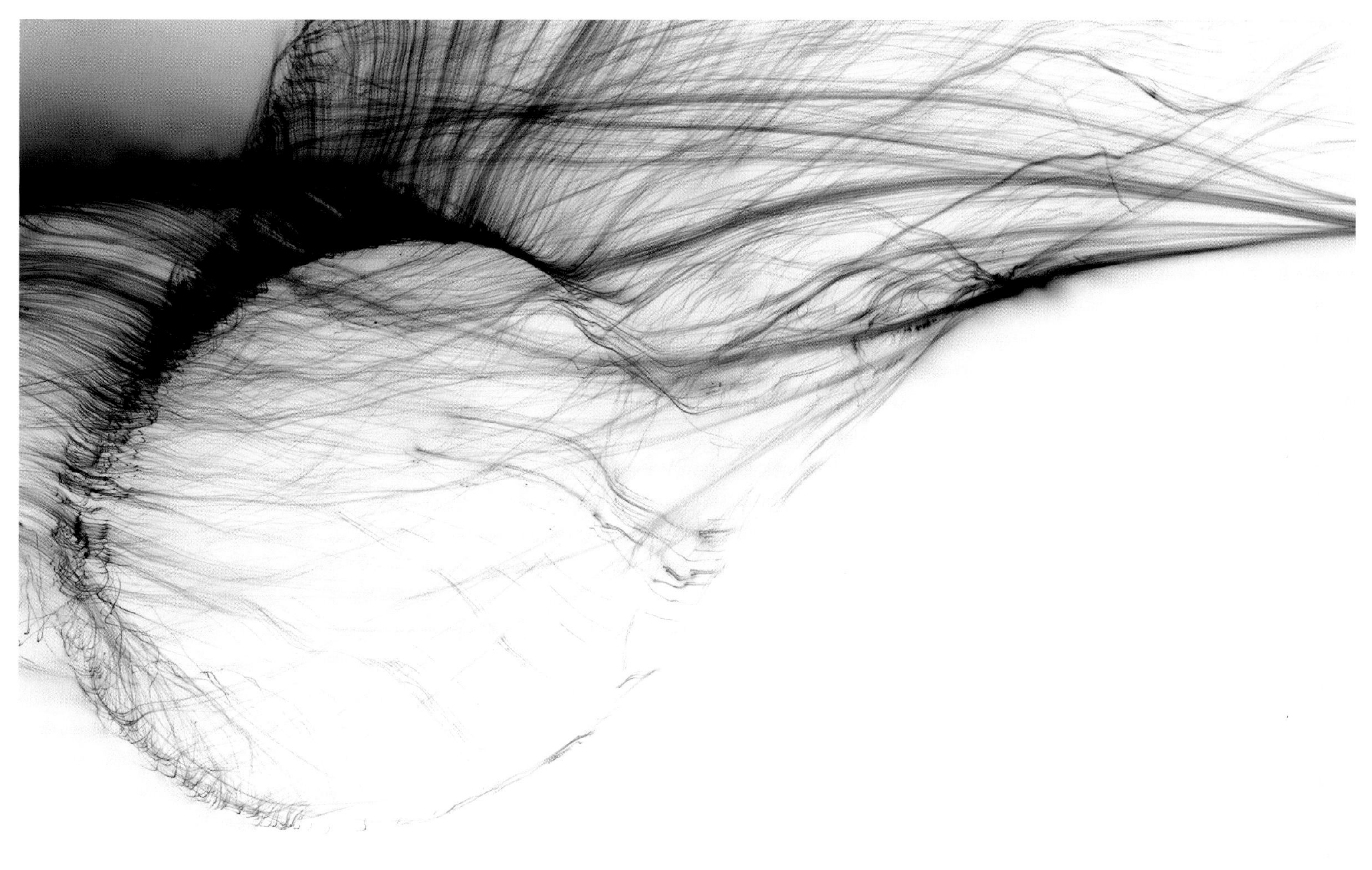

William Eggleston
Untitled from "Memphis," 1976

Courtesy of Cheim & Read, New York

Wolfgang Tillmans
Freischwimmer 55, 2004
C-Print mounted on Sintra in an artist's frame
181 x 237 x 6 cm
Courtesy of Galerie Daniel Buchholz, Cologne

Tham & Videgård Hansson Arkitekter
Refurbishment of an apartment at Humlegården, Stockholm, 2008
Multi-colored parquet on floors and walls

Hella Jongerius
Artificial vase Vert "#4," Collection "Natura Design Magistra," 2009
Vase: green glass, white terracotta
Flowers: blown glass, leather
H 116 cm (total dimension)
Numbered unique piece
Courtesy of Galerie Kreo, Paris

Raw-Edges, Shay Alkalay
Stack, 2008
H 180 cm
Chest of drawers with flexible elements
Manufacturer: Established & Sons

Arik Levy
Rock Fusion Soft, 2008
Polyethylene structure with fabric upholstery
Limited edition
Manufacturer: Ldesign

Richard Woods
Wrongwoods, 2007
Woodblock print pattern
Chest of drawers designed by Sebastian Wrong
L 109.2 x W 50.8 x H 73.6 cm
Manufacturer: Established & Sons

Shaan Syed
Shoegazer Number Three, 2008
Oil and polyfilla on canvas
183 x 153 cm
Courtesy of Galerie Michael Janssen, Berlin

Carsten Höller
Reindeer, 2008
Lime Biresin, blue glass eyes, horn
10 x 56 x 28 cm
Detail

Courtesy of Carsten Höller and Esther Schipper, Berlin

Anselm Reyle
Untitled, 2005
Mixed media on canvas, acrylic glass
234 x 199 x 20 cm
DaimlerChrysler Contemporary

Courtesy of Galerie Giti Nourbakhsch

Jaime Hayón
Green Chicken, 2006
Lacquered fiberglass
L 100 x W 40 x H 121 cm

Schulz & Schulz Architekten
Police station Chemnitz-Süd, Chemnitz, Germany, 2008
Redesign and refurbishment

Donald Judd
Untitled (Stack), 1967
New York, Museum of Modern Art (MoMA)
Lacquer on galvanized iron
12 units, each 22.8 x 101.6 x 78.7 cm, installed vertically with 22.8 cm intervals
Helen Achen Bequest (by exchange) and gift of Joseph Helman

Massimiliano & Doriana Fuksas
Kensington Gardens, 2008
Installation at the Venice Architecture Biennale
View of exhibition container

Anish Kapoor
Wave, 2003
Aluminum, paint
D 46.5, ø 226 cm
Courtesy of Lisson Gallery

Katharina Fritsch
Elefant (Elephant), 1987
Polyester, wood, paint
160 x 420 x 380 cm

Courtesy of Matthew Marks Gallery, New York

Sylvie Fleury
Mushroom (BC T 500 Gemini 0006), 2005
Fiberglass, metallic car paint
H 130, ø 110 cm, 2 parts
Unique
© Sylvie Fleury
Courtesy of Sprüth Magers Berlin London
and Thaddaeus Ropac Salzburg – Paris

Mattia Bonetti
Heather, 2007
Chest of drawers made of fiberglass, metallic paint
H 99 x W 130 x D 65 cm
Editions David Gill, limited to 8 + 2 P. + 2 A.P.
© 2009, ProLitteris, Zurich
Courtesy of David Gill Galleries

Mass Studies, Minsuk Cho
Ann Demeulemeester Shop, Seoul, 2007
Vertical gardens, colored exposed concrete, internal staircase covered with moss
Staircase and external view

Zaha Hadid
Gyre, 2006
Polyester, resin
L 212 x W 142 x H 67.5 cm
Edition of 12
Manufacturer: Established & Sons

Hella Jongerius
Polder Sofa, 2005
L 226 to 333 x W 95.9 to 100 x H 78 cm
Manufacturer: Vitra

BarberOsgerby
Iris 1200, 2008
Anodised aluminum, glass
H 39, ø 120 cm
Limited edition of 12
Manufacturer: Established & Sons

Hella Jongerius
Office Pets, Beetle, 2007
Leather, polyurethane
H 195, ø 62 cm
Edition of 8 each for Vitra Edition
in cooperation with Galerie Kreo, Paris
Manufacturer: Vitra

David Chipperfield Architects
"City of Justice," Barcelona, 2008
Court-house and judicial offices
Concrete, pigmented in pastel shades

Joachim Grommek
B4, 2007
Lacquer, acrylic, oil, primer
on laminated chipboard
65 x 50 cm
Private collection, Ravensburg
Courtesy of VOUS ETES ICI, Amsterdam

BarberOsgerby
Lanterne Marine, 2009
Hand blown glass, anodised aluminum frame
Limited edition
Manufacturer: Venini

Tom Dixon
Copper Shade, 2005
Polycarbonate, copper
H 41, ø 45 cm
Manufacturer: Tom Dixon

Studio Job
The Last Supper, Gospel, 2009
Corroded foundry iron
145 x 86 x 90 cm
Edition of 2 + 1 A.P.
Collection ING art collection
Detail of sculpture

Tilo Schulz
Intarsie, 2006
Wood veneer marquetry
40 x 70 cm
Courtesy of Dogenhaus Galerie, Leipzig

William Eggleston
Untitled, 1971
© Eggleston Artistic Trust
Courtesy of Cheim & Read, New York

Jurgen Bey, Studio Makkink & Bey
Ear Chair, 2008 (first design from 2002)
L 110 x W 78 x H 149 cm
Manufacturer: Proof

Valerio Olgiati
House for a Musician, Scharans, Switzerland 2007
Red-stained concrete

Maarten Baas
Plastic Chair in Wood, 2008
Carved elm wood, varnish
H 78 x W 55 x D 56 cm
Courtesy of Contrasts Gallery, Shanghai

FORM Kouichi Kimura Architects
House of Vision, Shiga, Japan, 2008
Private residence

Ron Arad
Do-Lo-Rez, 2008
Wood frame, foam
Manufacturer: Moroso

Thomas Demand
Archiv (Archive), 1995
C-Print/Diasec
183.5 x 233 cm
© Thomas Demand/2009, ProLitteris, Zurich
Courtesy of Sprüth Magers Berlin London

Arik Levy
Rock Wood, 2007
Wenge wood
Limited edition
Manufacturer: Ldesign
Courtesy of ROVE, London

Tilo Schulz
Intarsie, 2008
Wood veneer marquetry
60 x 60 cm
Courtesy of Dogenhaus Galerie, Leipzig

ACHROMATIC

Sirous Namazi
Interior, 2007
7 Lambda prints mounted with acrylic glass and aluminum
3 panels, each 89 x 110 cm, and 4 panels, each 110 x 89 cm
Edition of 6
Courtesy of Sirous Namazi and Galerie Nordenhake
Berlin/Stockholm

Front
Tensta Chair, 2005
Leather seat, plastic chair
Part of an installation at Tensta Konsthall, Stockholm, 2005

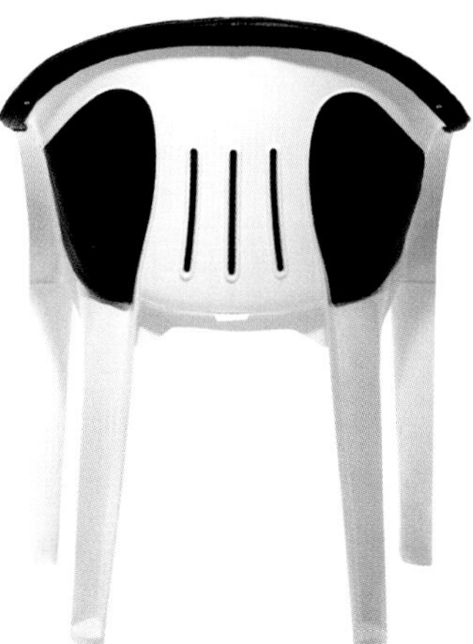

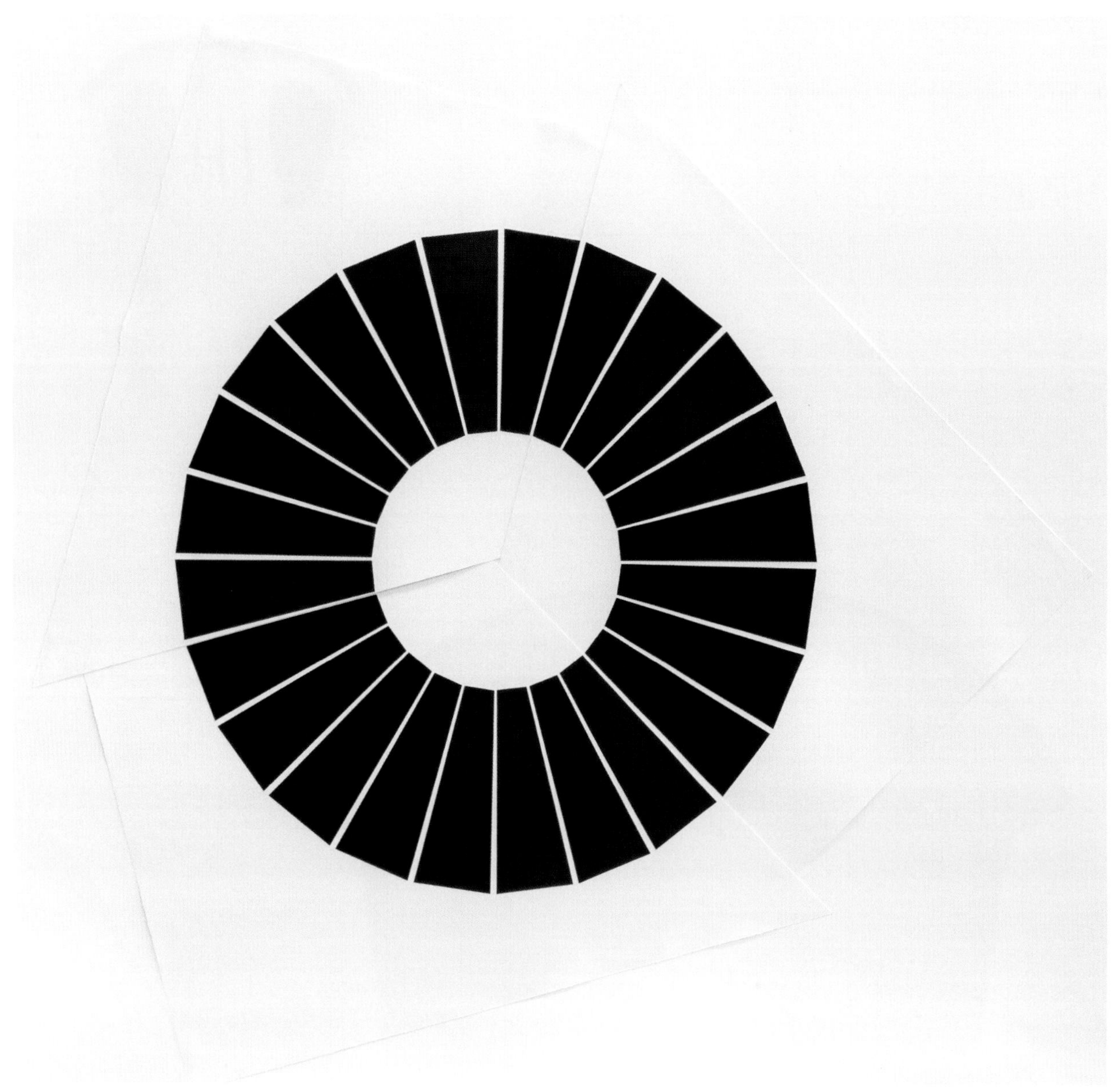

Olafur Eliasson
***The black colour circle*, 2008**
From *The colour circle series*, part 3
Color gravure
171 x 175 cm
Courtesy of Olafur Eliasson; neugerriemschneider, Berlin;
Niels Borch Jensen Galerie und Verlag, Berlin;
Tanya Bonakdar Gallery, New York

Katharina Fritsch
Schwarzer Schirm (Black Umbrella), 2004
Carbon, aluminum, plastic, lacquer
H 120, ø 100 cm

Courtesy of Matthew Marks Gallery, New York

Studio Job
Pyramid (mould), 2008
Mixed media, wax
Approx. 45 x 65 x 150 cm

Maison Martin Margiela
Garment from the MMM 20th anniversary show
Spring/summer 2009
Runway image

Jaime Hayón
Horse Vase, 2007
Ceramics
W 43.18 x H 34.98 cm
Manufacturer: Bosa Ceramiche

Maarten Baas
Smoke, 2004
Burnt furniture, epoxy finish
Original design: Ettore Sottsass' Carlton room divider, 1981
H 196 x W 190 x D 40 cm
Courtesy of Moss, New York

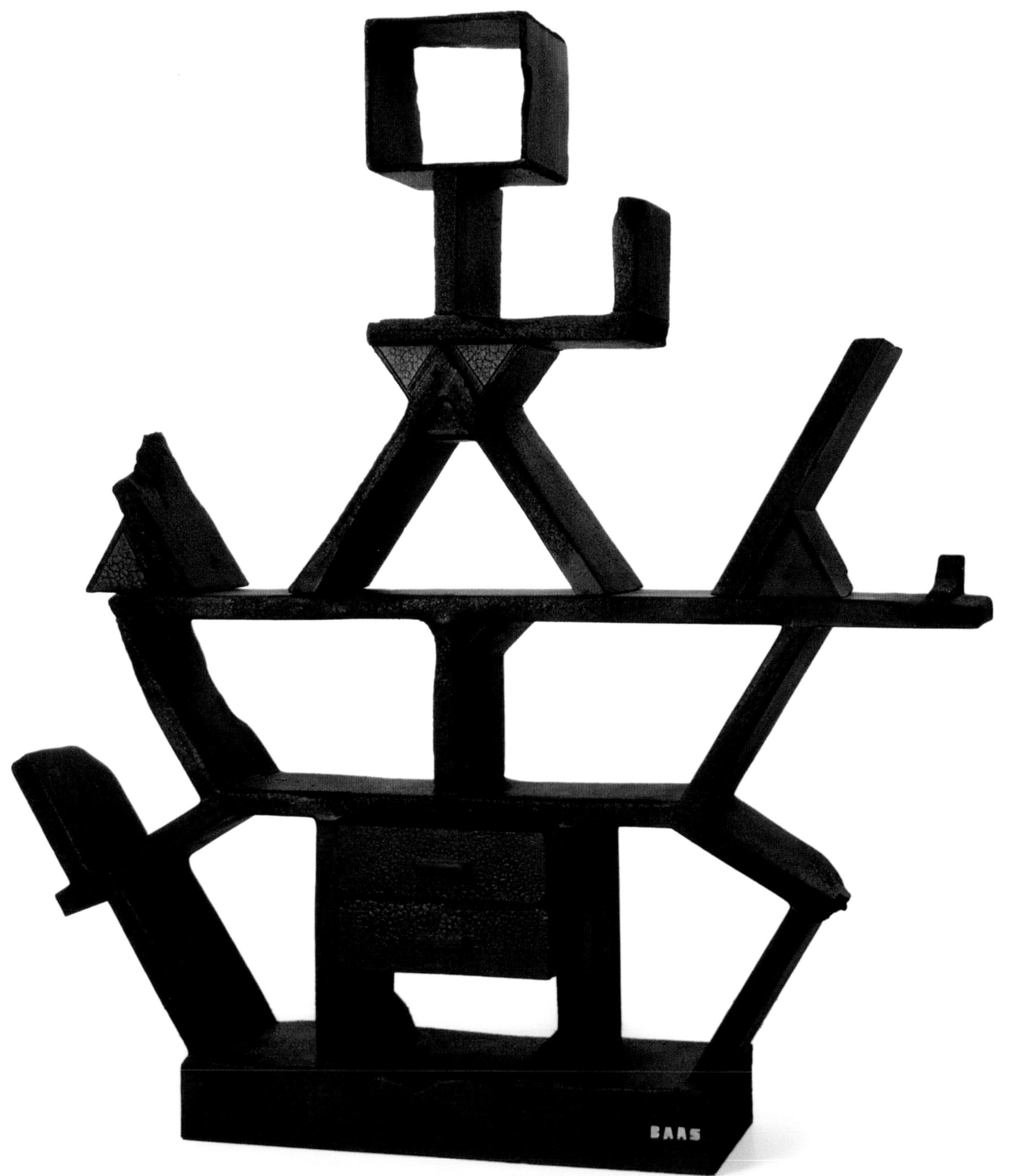
BAAS

Peter Haimerl
Das Schwarze Haus (The Black House), Krailing, Germany 2006
Remodelling of a housing-estate residence built in the 1930s

BLESS
Fat Knit Hammock, 2007
(Collection BLESS N°28 Climate Confusion Assistance)
White cotton canvas base, black fat knit inlay
Courtesy of the Musée d'Art Contemporain Genève

BLESS
Car Cover (Collection BLESS N°35 Automatica), 2008
Cotton fabric
Exclusively created for *Intersection* Magazine

Konstantin Grcic
Landen, 2007
Steel profile, metal grillage, rubber
L 262 x W 262 x H 130 cm
Edition of 12 for Vitra Edition
Manufacturer: Vitra

Andreas Exner
Schwarze Jacke (Black Jacket), 1992
Fabric, sewed
Approx. 80 x 57 cm

Courtesy of Galerie Horst Schuler, Düsseldorf

BarberOsgerby
Aluminum Zero-In, 2005
Mirror-polished, hand-pressed aluminum, glass
L 120 x D 120 x H 40 cm
Edition of 12
Manufacturer: Established & Sons

Maison Martin Margiela
Foxstole in party paper balls (Women)
Artisanal collection, spring/summer 2008
Party paper balls, hand dyed with China ink

Anselm Reyle
Untitled, 2008
Mixed media on canvas, acrylic glass
143 x 121 x 18.5 cm
Private collection
© 2009, ProLitteris, Zurich
Courtesy of Gagosian Gallery, New York

Gerhard Richter
Grau (Gray), 1973
Oil on canvas
250 x 200 cm
Ströher Collection
(GR 334)

FORM Kouichi Kimura Architects
House of Inclusion, Shiga, Japan, 2009
Private residence

Studio Schellmann Furniture
Storage, 2008
Steel frame, Euro-Fix plastic boxes
Boxes: 32 x 40 x 60 or 32 x 14 x 60 cm
Unit of 6 boxes 80 x 136 x 60 cm
Courtesy of Schellmann Furniture, Munich – New York

Hella Jongerius
Grenouille table, Collection "Natura Design Magistra," 2009
Walnut wood and transparent enamel paint
H 120 x W 210 x D 105 cm (total dimension)
Numbered limited edition of 8 + 2 A.P. + 2 prototypes
Detail
Courtesy of Galerie Kreo, Paris

Front
Changing cupboard, 2007
A constantly transforming cupboard built out of rotating bill-boards

Nitzan Cohen
nan15, bookshelf, 2008
Sheet steel 0.2 cm, powder-coated
Each unit: W 46.8 x D 31.4 x H 19.2 cm
Manufacturer: nanoo by Faserplast

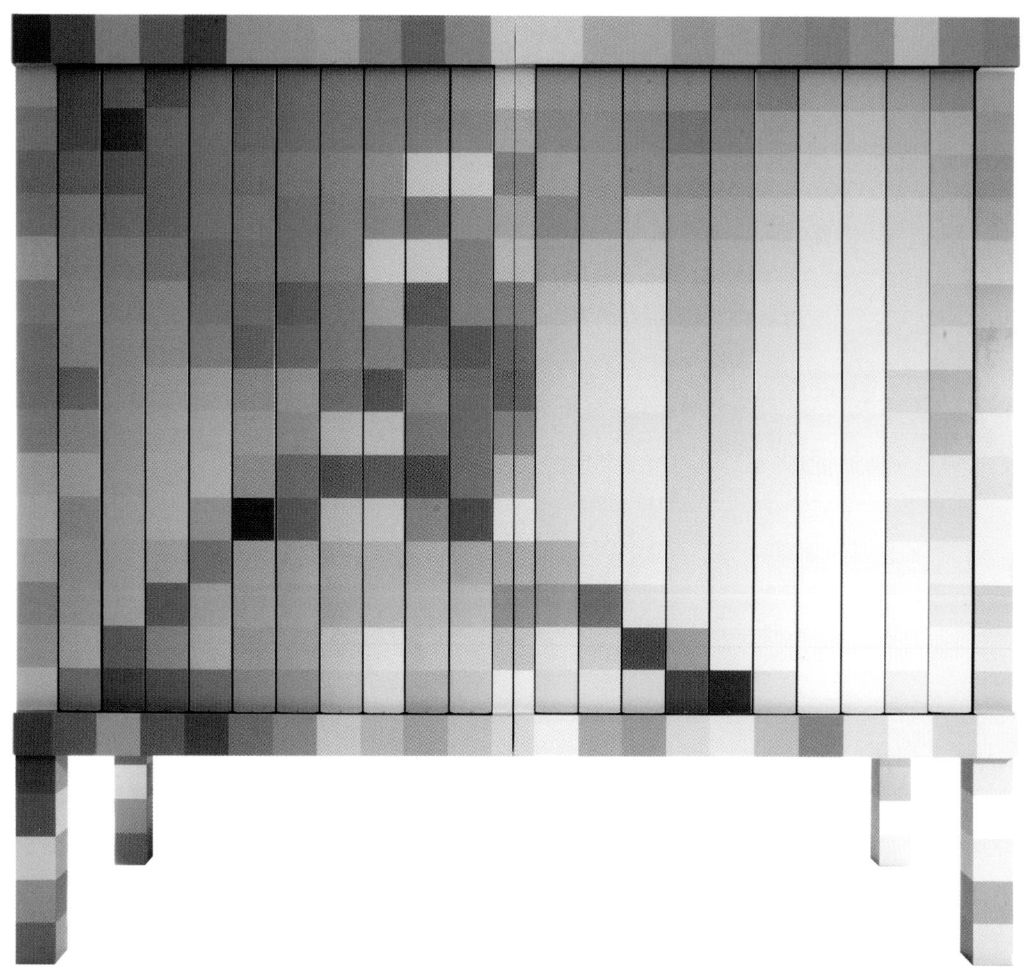

Valerio Olgiati
Das Gelbe Haus (The Yellow House), Flims, Switzerland, 1999
Fine white lime-wash coating
© Archiv Olgiati

Richard Woods
Wrongwoods, 2009
Woodblock print pattern
Chest of drawers designed by Sebastian Wrong
L 109.2 x W 50.8 x H 73.6 cm
Manufacturer: Established & Sons

Nendo
Cabbage Chair, 2008
Wax-impregnated waste paper from the pleated fabric industry
Designed for "XXIst Century Man" exhibition, 21_21 Design Sight, Tokyo

Saskia Diez
Papier (Paper), 2009
Tyvek®, light-weight robust synthetic paper
49 x 25 x 32 cm, weight 135 gr

Hiroshi Nakamura & NAP Architects
House SH, Tokyo, 2005
Reinforced concrete structure with cement mortar, finished with AEP paint

Konstantin Grcic
Diana F, 2002
Side table
Powder-coated steel sheet
44 x 53 x 25 cm
Manufacturer: ClassiCon

Maison Martin Margiela
Elastic Jacket (Women)
Artisanal collection, spring/summer 2008
White elastic bands in various shapes
and shades of color

Tokujin Yoshioka
Paper Cloud, 2009
Sofa, prototype in paper
L 97 x W 97 x H 60 cm
Manufacturer: Moroso

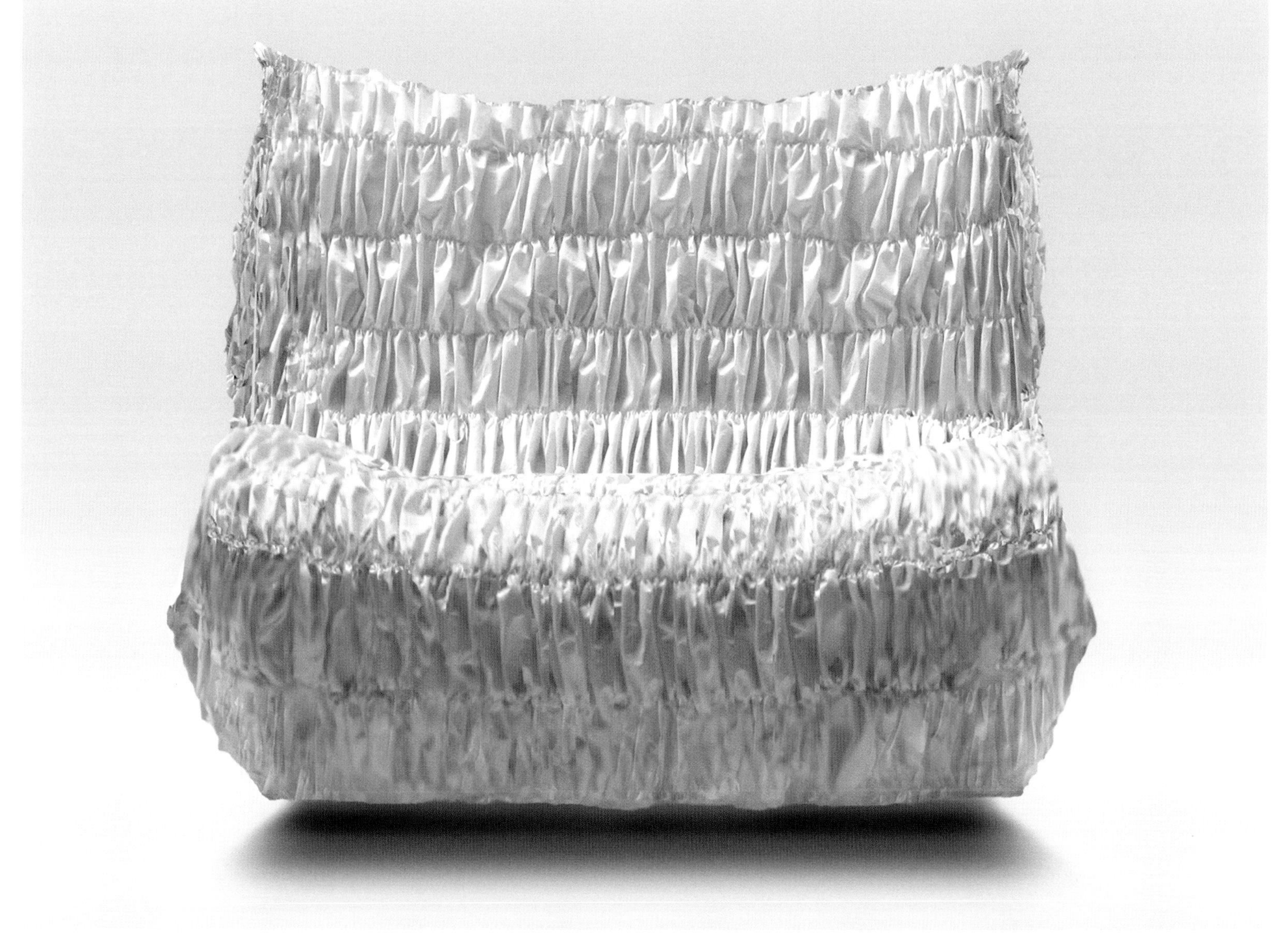

Jaime Hayón
Armchair, BD Showtime Collection, 2006
W 90 x D 82 x H 168 cm
Manufacturer: Bd Barcelona Design

Katharina Grosse
This Is No Dogshit, 2007
Acrylic on glass, metal, brick, cobblestone
Exhibition view: "Franchise" Foundation, Leeuwarden, 2007

Studio Job
Cake of Peace, Biscuit, 2006
Biscuit porcelain
W 25 x D 25 x H 22 cm
Collection Groninger Museum
Manufacturer: Royal Tichelaar Makkum

Jurgen Bey
Slow Car, 2007
Polyurethane, steel structure
L 250 x W 180 x H 250 cm
Prototype for Vitra Edition
Manufacturer: Vitra

Stefan Diez
Couch, 2005
Foam-Ergofill filling, canvas covering
L 155 x W 75 x H 73 cm
Manufacturer: elmarflötotto

Olafur Eliasson
***The white colour circle*, 2008**
From *The colour circle series*, part 3
Color gravure
171 x 174 cm
Courtesy of Olafur Eliasson; neugerriemschneider, Berlin; Niels Borch Jensen Galerie und Verlag, Berlin; Tanya Bonakdar Gallery, New York

MULTICHROMATIC

Liam Gillick
Shelf System A, 2008
Powder-coated aluminum
Each 10 x 20 x 100 cm
Edition of 100
Courtesy of Liam Gillick and Schellmann Furniture, Munich – New York

Beat Zoderer
Transparente Ordnung (Transparent Order), 1991
3 plastic sleeves, stuck into each other
22.5 x 22 cm
© 2009, ProLitteris, Zurich
Courtesy of Beat Zoderer

Astrid Bornheim Architektur

Facade of the Eternit headquarters, Heidelberg, 2006

Redesign of a facade for a building constructed in 1964
in cooperation with dko architekten, Berlin
Fiber-cement slabs

Michael Reiter
Komet, 2007
Ribbonbands, sewed
Approx. 53 x 36 x 11 cm
Courtesy of Galerie Martina Detterer

Ellsworth Kelly
Spectrum IV, 1967
New York, Museum of Modern Art (MoMA)
Oil on canvas, 13 panels
297.2 x 297.2 cm
Mrs. John Hay Whitney Bequest and The Sidney and Harriet Janis Collection (both by exchange), and gift of Irving Blum

Imi Knoebel
Fishing Pink, 2009
Acrylic, aluminum
300 x 450.4 x 16 cm

Gerhard Richter
192 Farben (192 Colors), 1966
Oil on canvas
200 x 150 cm
(GR 136)

Katharina Grosse
Holey Residue, 2006
Acrylic on earth, canvas, wall
379 x 667 x 464 cm
Exhibition view: "Holey Residue," De Appel, Amsterdam 2006

Keisuke Fujiwara
5 pm in the autumn [table high], 2002
5 pm in the summer -windy- [table low], 2003
From the "Titanium Work Series," beginning 2001
Anodised titanium

Kostas Murkudis
96dresses, 2008
Silk

Joachim Grommek
#80 (Polaroid), 2006
Lacquer, acrylic, oil, primer
on laminated chipboard
50 x 50 cm
Private collection, Germany
Courtesy of VOUS ETES ICI, Amsterdam

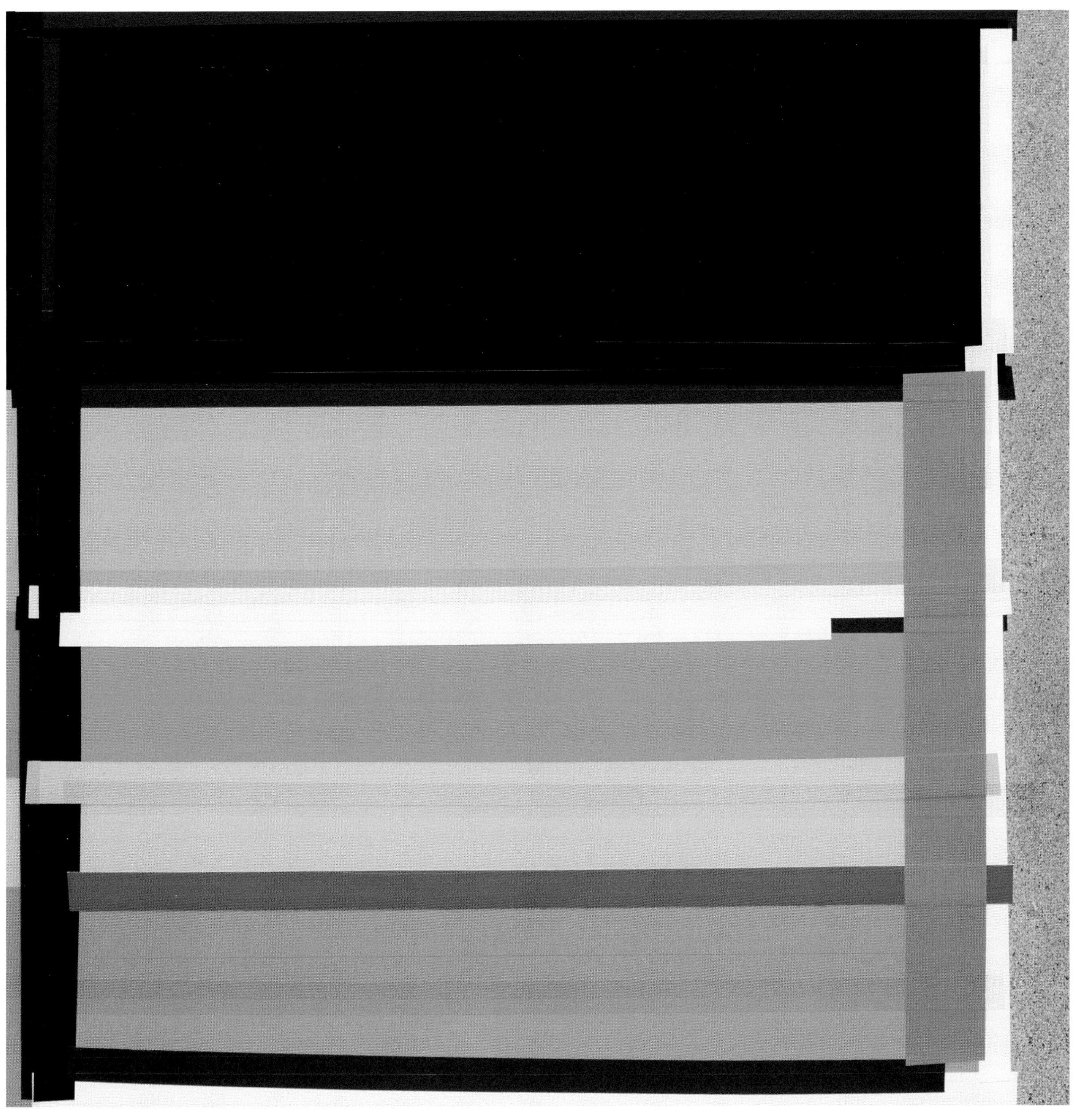

Committee, Clare Page & Harry Richardson
Victory from the "Kebab Lamps" series, 2006
Selection of found objects, skewered

Carsten Höller
Tortoreto Ondablu, 2007
C-Print mounted on aluminum
92.5 x 124 cm (image size), 117.5 x 149 cm
(photographic paper size)

Courtesy of Carsten Höller and Esther Schipper, Berlin

Scholten & Baijings
Colour Plaid 03, 2005
Merino wool and cotton
140 x 180 cm and 280 x 260 cm
Manufacturer: Scholten & Baijings and De Ploeg

Olav Christopher Jenssen
Relevance (From the Protagonist), 2007/2008
Acrylic on canvas
W 245 x H 245 cm

Courtesy of Galleri Riis, Oslo

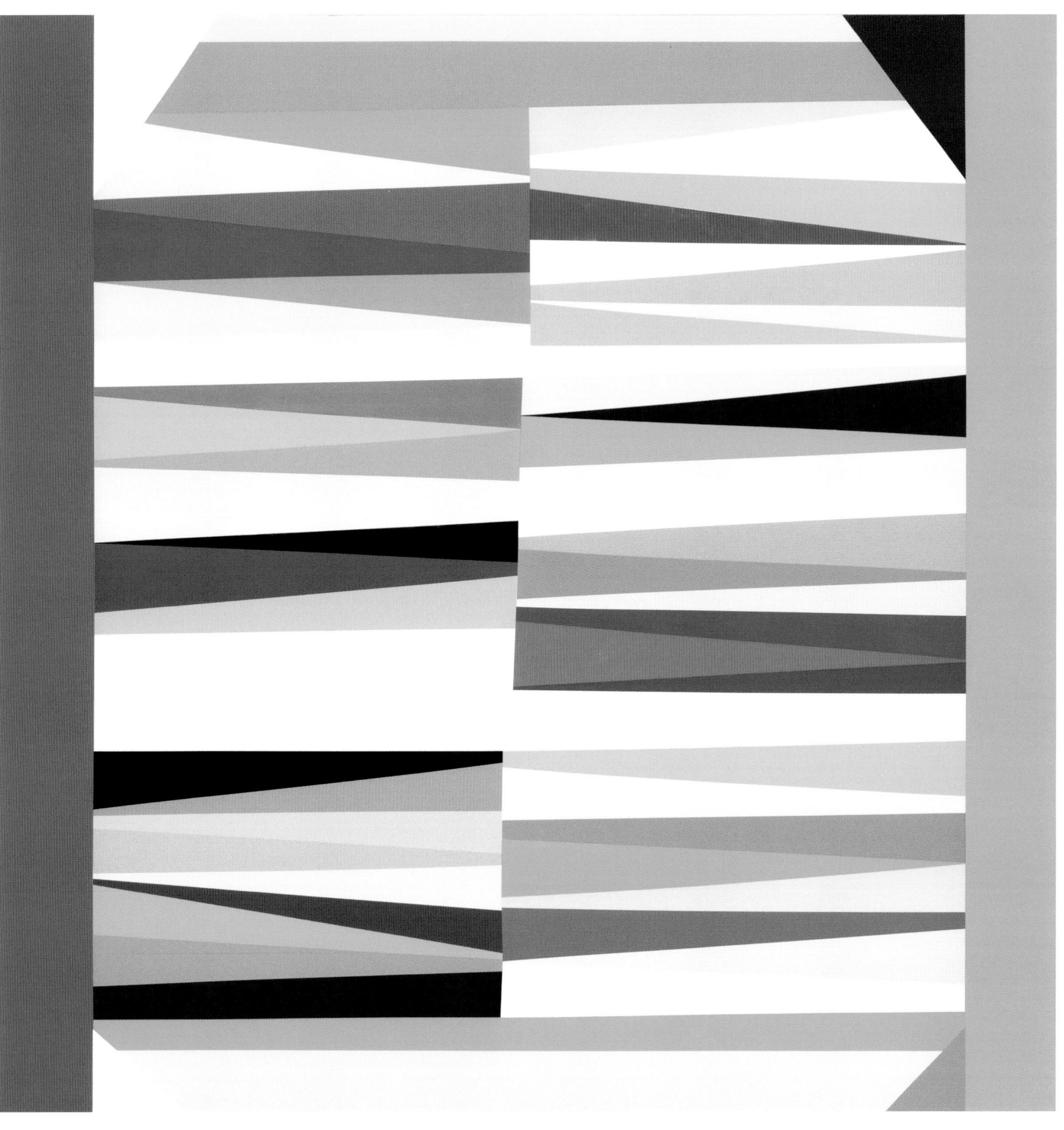

Jean Nouvel
Torre Agbar, Barcelona, 2005
Aluminum glass facade in 40 different shades of color

Sirous Namazi
Untitled (Modules), 2007
Iron, enamel paint
168 x 175 x 28 cm
Courtesy of Sirous Namazi and Galerie Nordenhake
Berlin/Stockholm

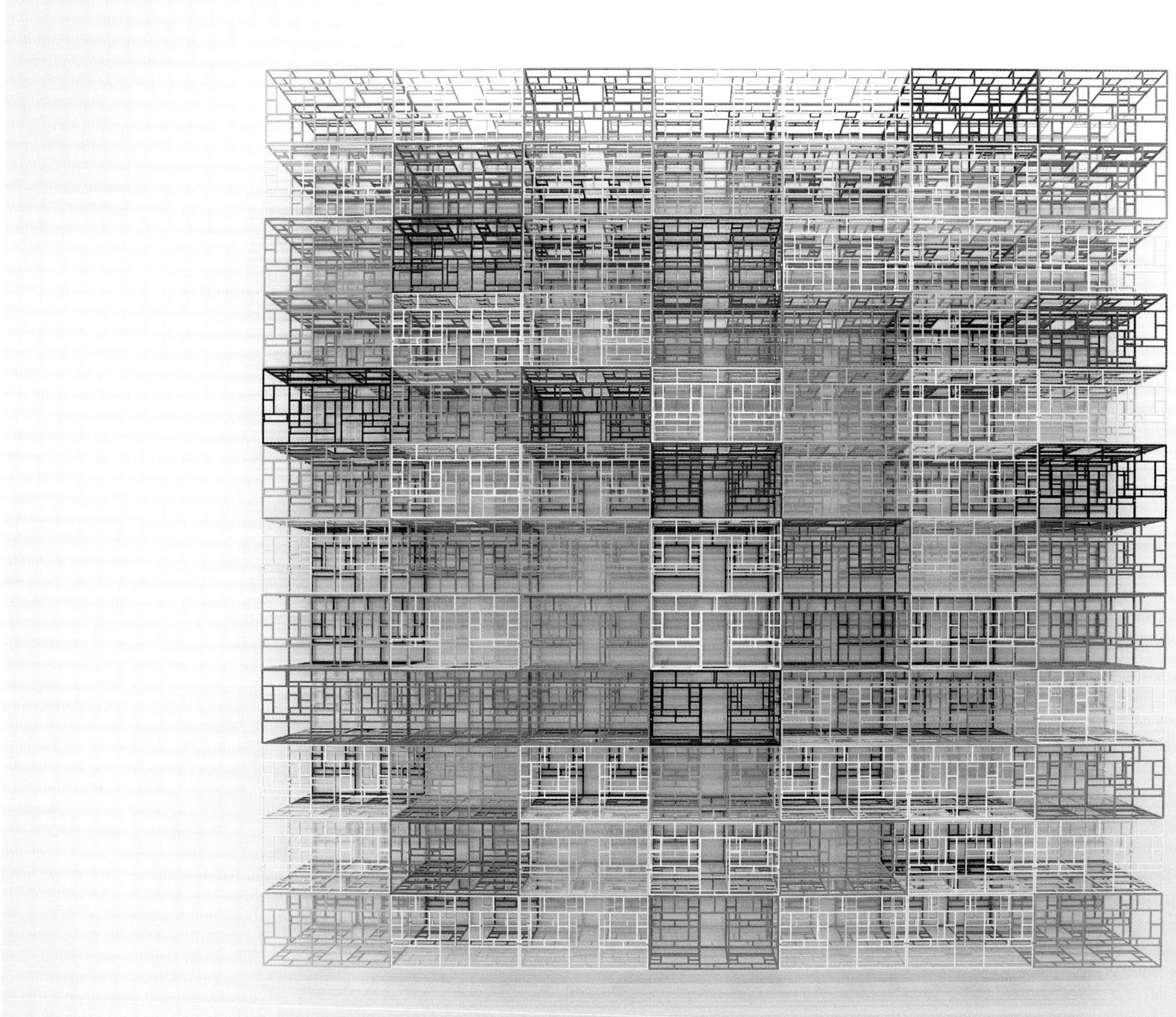

Liam Gillick
RELIEVED DISTRIBUTED, 2007
Powder-coated aluminum
20 elements, each L 200 x W 3 x D 15 cm, each mounted with a 4 cm gap
L 200 x W 136 x D 15 cm (total dimension)
Unique
Courtesy of Liam Gillick and Casey Kaplan, New York

John Baldessari
Beast (Orange) Being Stared At: With Two Figures (Green, Blue), 2004
Three-dimensional digital archival print with acrylic paint on Sintra, Dibond, and Gatorfoam panels
305.8 x 354 x 8.9 cm
Courtesy of John Baldessari, Marian Goodman Gallery, New York and Paris, and Sprüth Magers Berlin London

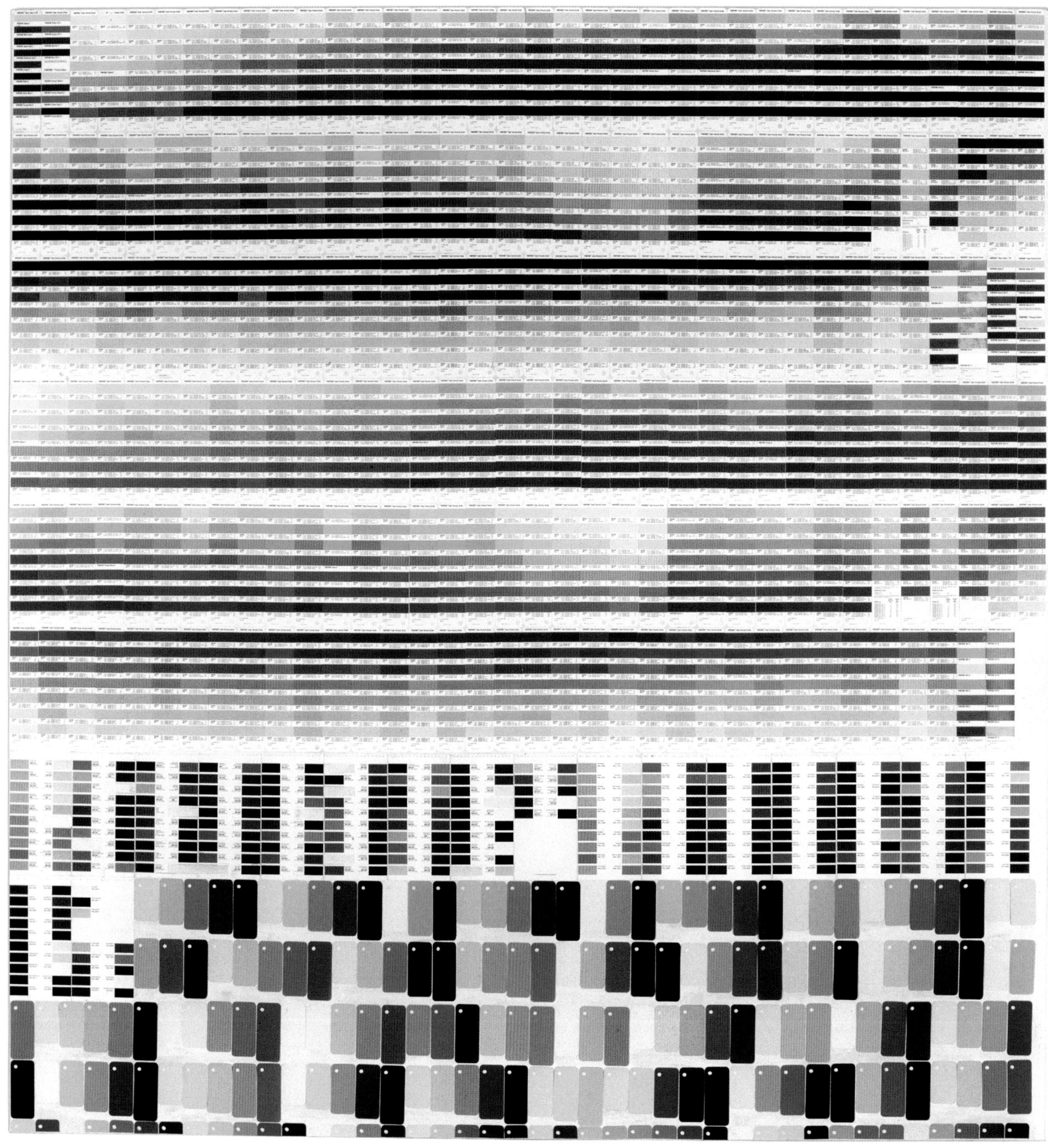

Beat Zoderer
RAL and Pantone, 1995
RAL and Pantone color charts on canvas, glued
190 x 180 cm

Courtesy of Beat Zoderer

BLESS
Hand knitted Sweater Degradé (Collection BLESS N°19 Uncool), 2003
Hand knitted jumper with color shade degradé, made out of wool
Courtesy of BLESS

GIOTTO TURBOCOLOR

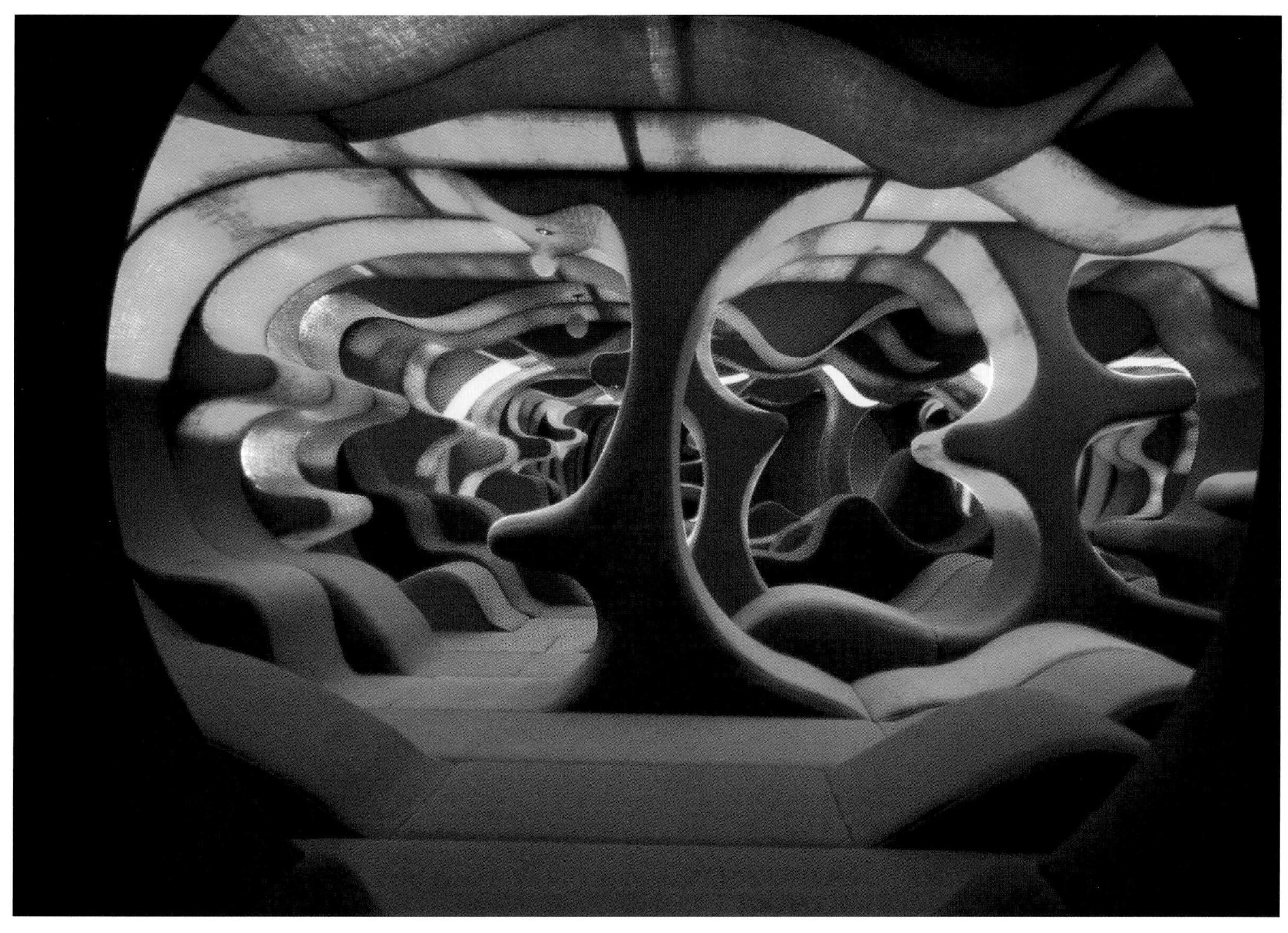

Fernando Brízio
Painting With Giotto #1, Vase, 2005
Faience and felt-tips
H 39, ø 29 cm
Limited edition of 20 + 2 A.P. + 2 prototypes
Courtesy of Galerie Kreo, Paris

Verner Panton
Visiona 2, 1970
Installation on a pleasure boat for the Cologne furniture fair
Client: Bayer

Job

Studio Job
The Crucifixion, Gospel, 2009
Polychrome hand blown glass, lead, Indian rosewood
367 x 217 x 15 cm
Edition of 1 + 1 A.P.
Collection Zuiderzee Museum

Liam Gillick
RESCINDED PRODUCTION, 2008
Powder-coated aluminum, transparent colored acrylic glass
L 240 x W 240 x H 200 cm
Unique
Courtesy of Liam Gillick and Casey Kaplan, New York

Committee, Clare Page & Harry Richardson
Love I, Love II, Love III from the "Evolution of Love" series, 2008
Porcelain
32 x 21 cm, 27 x 17 cm, 34 x 17 cm
Manufacturer: Lladro

Gerhard Richter
1024 Farben (1024 Colors), 1974
Lacquer on canvas
299 x 299 cm
Ströher Collection
(GR 355-1)
© Gerhard Richter

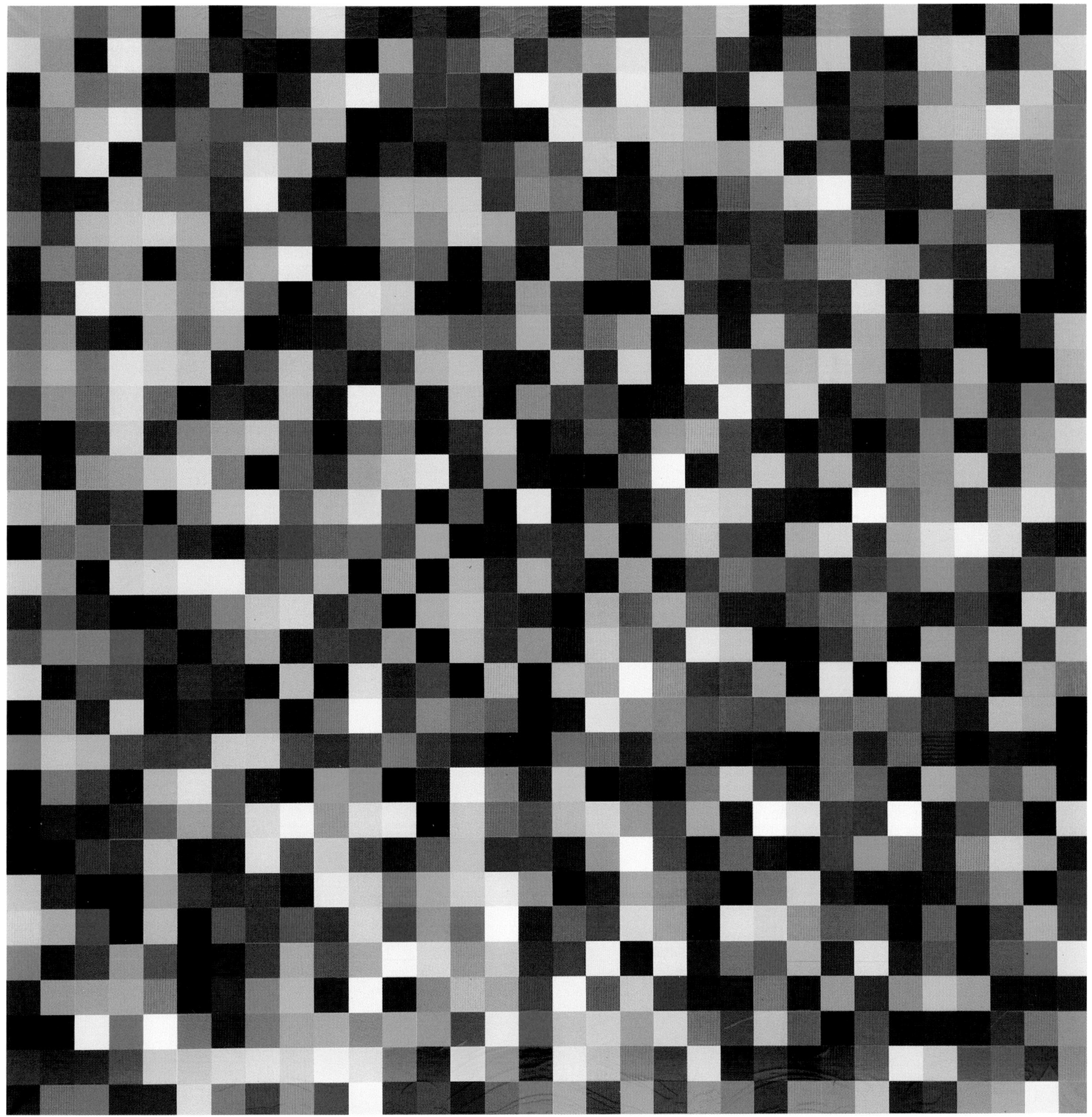

Nendo
Cabbage Chair, 2008
Wax-impregnated waste paper from
the pleated fabric industry
Designed for "XXIst Century Man" exhibition,
21_21 Design Sight, Tokyo

Peter Zimmermann
Untitled, 2008
60 x 45 cm
Epoxy on canvas

Courtesy of Galerie Michael Janssen, Berlin

Maison Martin Margiela
Kite Tunic
Artisanal collection, spring/summer 2009
Tunic made from a kite, embroidered with
20 m of rayon fringes

Peter Zimmermann
Swiss II, 2005
200 x 145 cm
Epoxy on canvas

Courtesy of Galerie Michael Janssen, Berlin

Sauerbruch Hutton

Experimental Factory, Magdeburg, Germany, 2001

Research center
Building complex covered with a curved,
striped metal roof in orange, pink and silver-gray

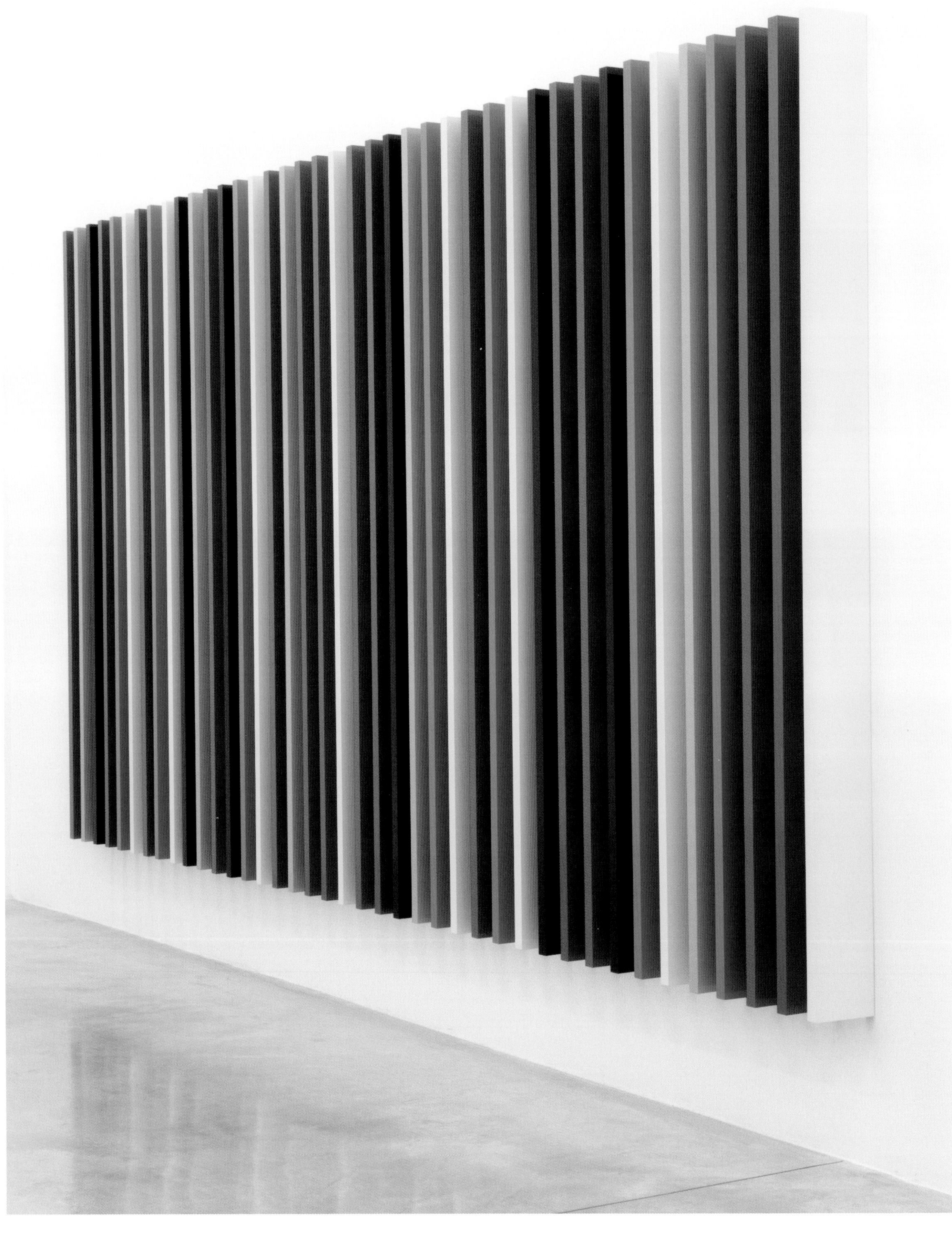

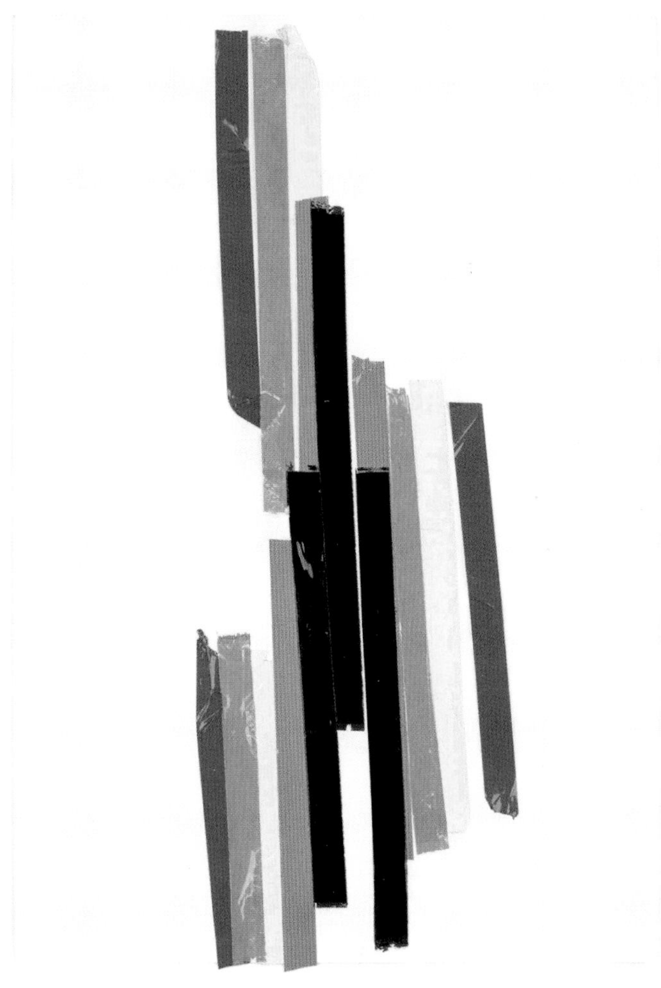

Liam Gillick
Between Kalmar and Udevalla, 2008
Powder-coated aluminum
40 elements, each L 200 x W 3 x D 15 cm, each mounted with a 7 cm gap
L 200 x W 393 x D 15 cm (total dimension)
Unique
Courtesy of Liam Gillick and Casey Kaplan, New York

Charlotte Posenenske
Streifenbild (Striped Picture), 1965
Colored tape on paper
34 x 24 cm
Signed and dated: "CMP 65," Museum Ludwig, Cologne

Richard Woods
Stone Clad Cottages, 2008
Green Lodge Cottages, Kettering
Courtesy of Fermyn Woods

Beat Zoderer
Kringel Nr. 1 (Squiggle no. 1), 2005
Acrylic prime varnish on metal strips, curled
ø 70 cm

Courtesy of Beat Zoderer

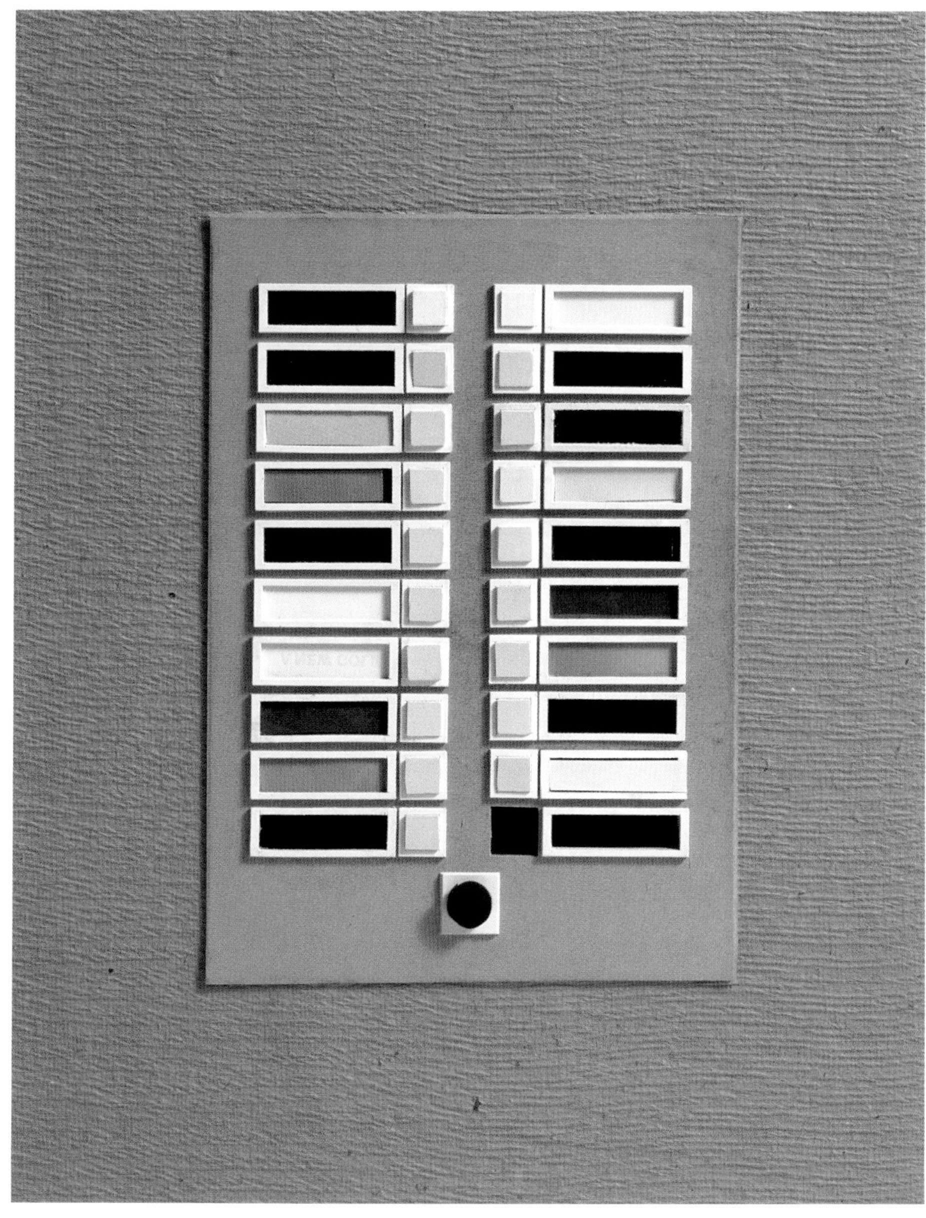

Sauerbruch Hutton
Brandhorst Museum, Munich, 2008
Facade consisting of 36,000 vertically arranged ceramic rods in 23 different colors

Thomas Demand
Hinterhaus, 2005
C-Print/framed
26.9 x 21.5 cm

OFIS Arhitekti
Apartments on the Coast, Izola, Slovenia, 2005
Sun shades in various colors

Stefan Diez & Christophe de la Fontaine
Bent, 2006
Laser cut and bent aluminum,
epoxy powder-coated finish
L 93 x W 61 x H 69 cm
Manufacturer: Moroso

Mansilla+Tuñón
MUSAC Contemporary Art Museum
of Castilla y León, León, Spain, 2004
Facade of colored glass

Olav Christopher Jenssen
Weimar, 2005–2006
Acrylic on canvas
W 245 x H 245 cm

Courtesy of Galleri Riis, Oslo

Wolfgang Tillmans
paper drop (rainbow), 2006
C-Print, various sizes
Courtesy of Galerie Daniel Buchholz, Cologne

David Adjaye & Peter Saville
Kvadrat London Showroom, 2009
Stairway lined with a spectrum-colored glass balustrade

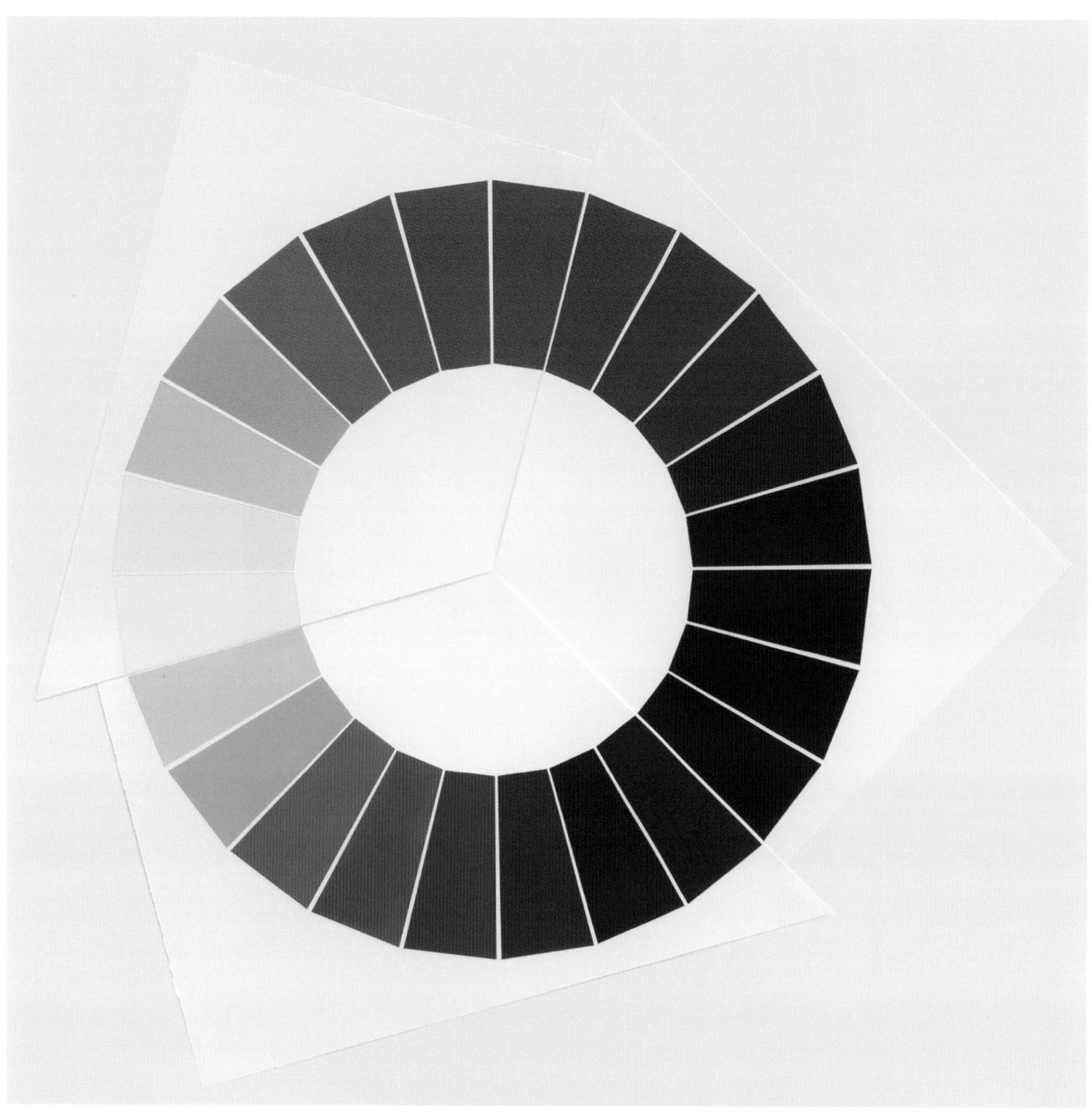

Olafur Eliasson
***The constant colour circle*, 2008**
From *The colour circle series*, part 1
Color gravure
168 x 175 cm
Courtesy of Olafur Eliasson; neugerriemschneider, Berlin;
Niels Borch Jensen Galerie und Verlag, Berlin;
Tanya Bonakdar Gallery, New York

Willy Müller Architects (WMA)
New Flower Market "Mercabarna-Flor," Barcelona, 2008
Zinc walls and roof clad with a continuous band
of colored panels

Anselm Reyle
Untitled, 2007
Mixed media on canvas, stainless steel frame
227 x 332 cm
Ovitz Family Collection, Los Angeles

Courtesy of Gagosian Gallery, New York

Michael Reiter
Container, 2007
Ribbon bands, sewed
Approx. 38 x 38 x 2 cm
Courtesy of Galerie Martina Detterer

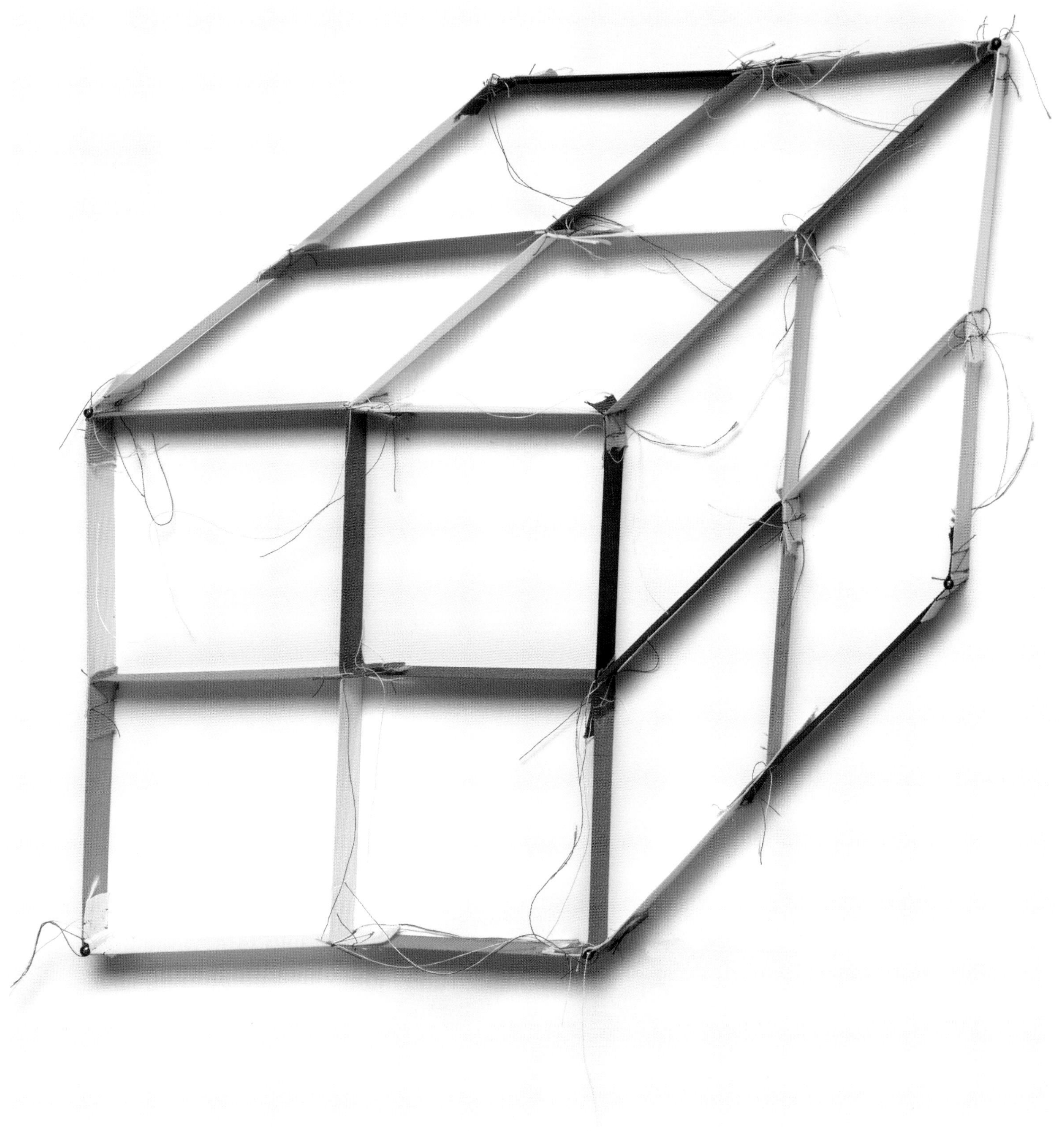

John Baldessari
Gavel, 1987
2 black-and-white photographs with vinyl paint, mounted on board
123.2 x 76.8 cm
Courtesy of John Baldessari, Marian Goodman Gallery,
New York and Paris, and Sprüth Magers Berlin London

Imi Knoebel
Ort – Blau Gelb Rot Rot, 2008
Acrylic, aluminum
302 x 300.5 x 150 cm
© Imi Knoebel/2009, ProLitteris, Zurich

CHROMA CHOICE

What draws the Bouroullec brothers to green tones? How do the architects Matthias Sauerbruch und Louisa Hutton create their finely nuanced facades? What inspires the Brazilian brothers Fernando and Humberto Campana to create their spectacular surfaces? What do trashy glosses mean for the artist Anselm Reyle? And how does Konstantin Grcic select his color spectrum? These are the questions explored in the chapter CHOICE. In five interviews specially given for CHROMA, designers, artists, and architects talk about their color concepts. In addition, renowned journalists have contributed three essays exploring the artistic and design approaches and motivations of Gerhard Richter, UNStudio, and Rupprecht Geiger.

It quickly becomes clear how important childhood experiences and early interests are for the perception of color. In particular the painter Anselm Reyle, who was already fascinated by abstract painting as a child, but also the designers Konstantin Grcic and Louisa Hutton, make clear just how significant certain aspects of their biographies have been for their sense of color today. While Grcic—who has made a particularly striking approach to color his own—makes the color spectrum of Lego and the gray of his hometown Wuppertal seminal elements of his work, Reyle and Hutton draw on the work of artists such as Blinky Palermo and the Dutch painters of the sixteenth century. The personal insights they allow us to be privy to show how different the worlds are that these artists and designers come from when it comes to color.

Fernando & Humberto Campana
"Color is determined by material"

1 Boa, 2002
Sofa
Manufacturer: edra

2 Scrigno, 2009
Cupboard
Manufacturer: edra

3 Segreto, 2009
Container
Manufacturer: edra

4 Brasilia, 2005
Side table
Manufacturer: edra

5 Vermelha, 1998
Armchair
Manufacturer: edra

Brazilian designers Fernando and Humberto Campana experiment with very different types of materials, ranging from the remains of the recycling process to stuffed toys, ropes, and scraps of leather. The colors of their designs are just as varied and bold, even if the brothers themselves prefer natural colors, as Fernando Campana says in the interview.

Are there any colors that have been part of your life since childhood?
I have always liked our national colors, the green and yellow of the Brazilian flag. These colors were long considered a sign of bad taste, and everybody wore T-shirts imprinted with the American or British flags. But I love them. We grew up in a rural area where green, as the color of nature, had a tremendous impact on our lives.

What role do natural colors play in the way you perceive color?
We live in the tropics. The summer sunlight makes the colors much brighter than any other place on earth. The color of the sky is quite different from the gray shades you see at other latitudes. If we lived in a hut in Norway for six months, we would probably have to reinvent our colors. The Brazilian landscape is also completely different, not monochrome, but full of colorful tropical flowers. You hardly see any intermediate shades in summer because the colors of the flowers, trees and fruits are so intense.

Do these impressions also play a role in the colors you choose?
Yes, natural colors flow into our work. Actually, it is always the material that determines the color. The choice of a particular color is always related to materials and their surfaces. We like using natural materials such as bamboo. Its light beige is a natural color. We prefer it if the material is a certain color that we can work with. For example, natural latex only comes in two or three colors. It is particularly beautiful when it dries in the sun—just like leather, which has incredibly beautiful, bold colors.

But you also use a lot of materials that have shiny, glittery surfaces and an artificial look.
These materials are a real challenge because they're very dominant. But we still try to liberate ourselves from the material at the start of the design process. We try to transform the material. It's only afterward that we address technical issues.

Are the colors used in your designs an expression of joie de vivre?
To a certain extent, yes. We recently took a picture of a man on the street carrying a stack of inflatable paddling pools and floating tires, and we called him the "inflatable man." He made a unique and highly amusing impression. Of course, you have to wonder whether this street vendor can really be happy having a gigantic piece of colored jewelry on his head. Color can be amusing or sarcastic, but that doesn't mean it's not a serious matter.

Should design be more colorful in general?
No, I don't think so. It depends on how a designer uses color and what materials are selected. Natural materials and shades can be as

1

2

3

4

5

6
7
8
9
10

6 Cipria, 2009
Sofa
Manufacturer: edra

7 Miraggio, 2009
Wall mirror
Manufacturer: edra

8 Zig Zag screen, 2001
Paravent
Manufacturer: edra

9 Jenette, 2005
Chair
Manufacturer: edra

10 Leatherworks, 2009
Armchair
Manufacturer: edra

Further illustrations:
pp. 123

beautiful as intense synthetic colors or even shiny ones. Color can be interpreted in different ways. Every buyer selects his or her favorite color in the store.

What role do the manufacturers play in selecting color?
To be honest, we suggested only a single color for our new collection "Shining for Edra." The company developed the color concept and selected the colors. Reflective materials and green—very amusing.

You don't select the colors of your designs yourselves?
We only present one option. In most cases, the color of the design we present is simply the color of the material we used to build the prototype, to test the material. In this respect chance also comes into play. The manufacturer offers us different color palettes, and we reach a decision together after creatively experimenting with preferences and aversions. What is at stake is the harmony of the design, gradations, texture. The materials offer a specific range of colors, and we try to pick the ones we can be happy with over the long term.

Are you sometimes surprised then by the colors of your designs when you see them at exhibitions or in your customers' spaces?
Sometimes there are custom-made items that surprise us—designs that were created with natural materials in mind and that were then manufactured in black for the showroom. But that's OK, customers get what they want in the store. There have been times, however, when I've called people up and said: "Give that back and I'll make you another one."

Interview: Markus Frenzl

Sauerbruch Hutton
"For us color is a tool"

1 Fire and Police Station, Berlin, 2004

2 GSW Headquarters, Berlin, 1999
Office building

3 Jessop West, Sheffield, UK, 2008
Faculty buildings

Louisa Hutton and Matthias Sauerbruch have used finely balanced color concepts to develop their own design language. Their work is characterized by color combinations rather than monochrome blocks. The main difficulty of this approach, says Louisa Hutton, is linking colors and materials to form a unified whole.

How did colors become so important to your work?
Both of us were strongly influenced by painting at an early stage. Matthias' father was a painter and had a studio in his home, and I became intensely interested in sixteenth-century Dutch painting at the age of fourteen. As our work together progressed, color developed into a major focus. At the end of the 1980s we took part in numerous competitions through our London office. However, the initial commissions we received were largely confined to upgrades and renovations. London townhouses are often very cramped and we found that color could be used very effectively in this context to expand spaces optically.

How do you deploy color today?
For us color is an additional tool—just like form and light. Our initial idea incorporates a general concept of a color or color group. Normally we draw on the NCS system, which comprises almost 2000 colors. The biggest challenge is to find a way to apply the desired color to the relevant material. We collect color samples, products, and other reference materials that can help us to communicate our concept to the firms or manufacturers responsible for making our concept a reality. They need to understand our color concept if they want to apply it, for instance, to glass or ceramics.

What connection do you see between colors and materials?
We try to find a profound material quality in the color and to link colored areas with the surface characteristics of the materials involved. At the Brandhorst Museum in Munich, for example, the surface structure of the ceramic rods can only be discerned from close up. From further away, the individual rods combine to form large areas of neutralized color, which creates the impression of a large abstract painting with three different color zones. The combination of materiality, color, and color composition produces a completely new, oscillating building surface.

How many tones are we talking about?
Actually only twenty-three. We organized them into three groups, which correspond to the gray scale categories of light, medium, and dark, and which we called "Bad Bruise," "Deep Peach" and "Rubens' Flesh." The Brandhorst Museum is one of a number of projects that reveal our preference for red tones. However, we altered the color groups at least ten times before arriving at the final colors. The color selection remained a dynamic process right up to the end. Colors influence one another, which means that in a process like this, the color concept as a whole needs to be in place before you give the green light for particular colors.

Do you develop your color palettes intuitively or on the basis of studies, surveys, and analyses?

2

1

3

4

6

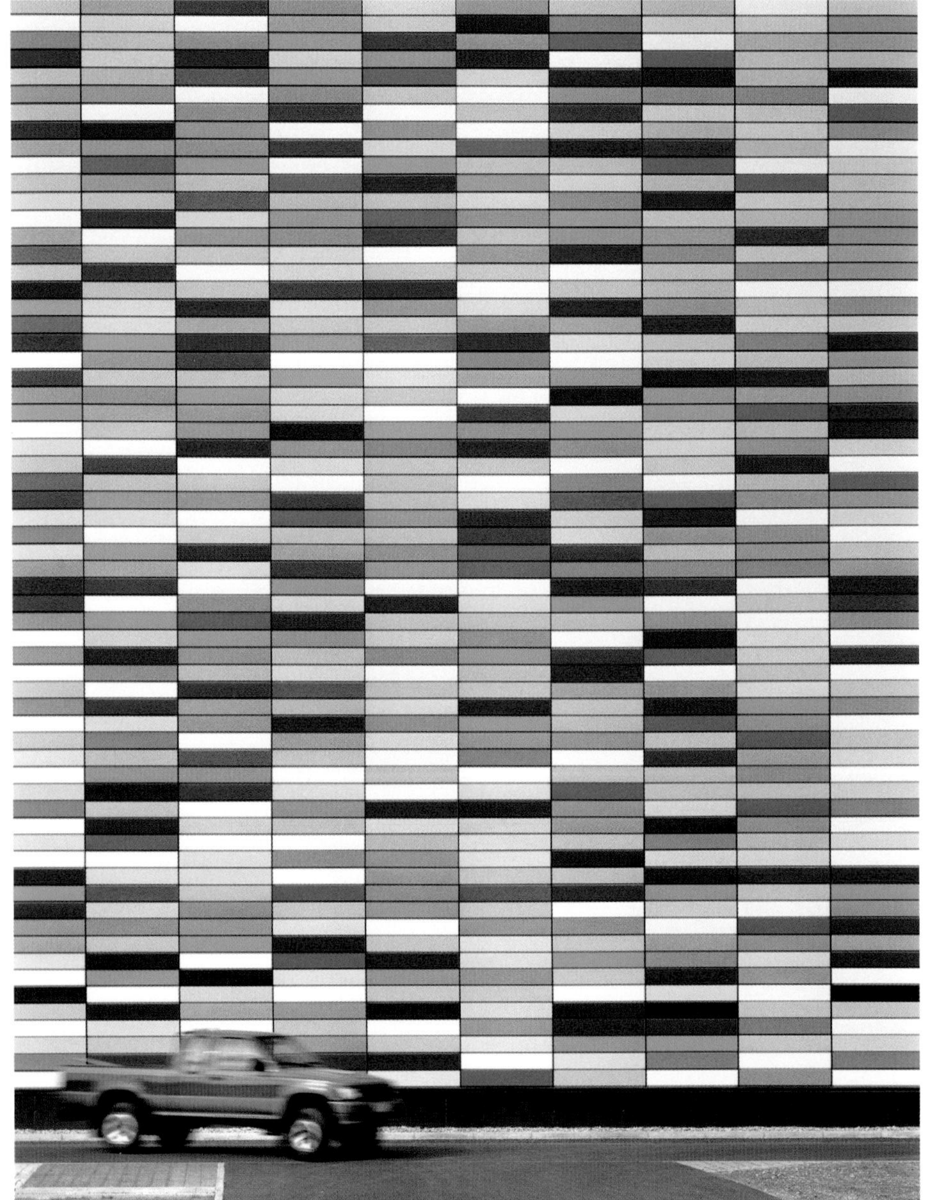

5

4, 5 Photonic Center, Berlin, 1998
Multifunctional building for laboratories, workshops, production facilities and offices

6 High-bay Warehouse Sedus Stoll, Dogern, Germany, 2003
Facade redesign

Further illustrations: pp. 254–255, 260

Intuitively, but we proceed very systematically and repeatedly try out different color combinations before we make a final decision. We use models and drawings to simulate the color palette and try to dissociate our emotions from our perception. Ideally, we like to test the colors in situ, using a model facade on a scale of 1:1.

Some of your architectural contemporaries regard colored buildings as a bit trendy and destined for a short life. What's your response?
The old idea of a timeless architecture is a little arrogant. Every building is an expression of its time and, just like people, has its own characteristics such as elegance or charm. These essential features are immune to fashion. I think that for many architects color is something that's considered after the fact, an additional element that doesn't really belong to the initial architectural concept—and there are many clients who share this point of view.

Modernism tended to regard color as subordinate. Are your color concepts liberating architecture from an outdated dogma?
No. Although we're critical of certain aspects of the modernist heritage, we see our work as generally within this tradition. As we see it, this includes the possibility of using color as a resource for creating space. We believe that the modernist credo of the "truth of the material" can be extended to include the potential offered by color.

Do you believe that too little attention is paid to color in the teaching of architecture?
Color should be a self-evident part of architectural practice, not analyzed as a scholarly or theoretical topic. To give one example, we don't consider color theories such as the one put forward by Johannes Itten to be particularly inspirational. It's probably more important to encourage architecture students to experiment with and investigate color in the same way as they experiment with models and sketches. Color is not a pseudo-artistic field within architecture but an extension of practical experience.

Interview: Markus Frenzl

Rupprecht Geiger
"High on red"

1 Weiß (synchron) zu Gelb-Orange, 2002
Acrylic, canvas
125 x 130 cm
(WV 914)
Geiger Archive

2 Wandplastik, 1971
Municipal court, entrance hall, Warendorf/Westphalia, Germany
Acrylic, aluminum
220 x 265 x 70 cm

3 Untitled, 1999
Silkscreen with original pigments/BFK, Rives, 300 gr
84 x 66 cm
40 + XII num., sig. Ex.
(WVG 199)

There have been many attempts to describe the effect of Rupprecht Geiger's paintings. Someone once called them "visible radioactivity." Others speak of "force fields," "meditation objects," and the "cosmic energy" that they emit. Still others focus on the sensation they create: that of sinking into an infinite, undefined space. Geiger's color-based paintings are evidently not easy to grasp conceptually. Art critic Thomas Wagner used an apt analogy when he compared the viewing experience with that of looking into the sun: if you look directly into the midday sun with your eyes closed—gazing at what would otherwise be an intolerable blinding light—you are filled with light and warmth and have an immediate, intense perception of color. Geiger's paintings are similar to the after-images or memory-related pictures that we see with our eyes closed: the perception is of pure color. And, indeed, what is at stake for Geiger is the act of seeing as a mental experience. "To really see color, you must close your eyes and imagine it," Geiger writes in the book *Farbe ist Element* (Color is Element). But how does he manage to allow the viewer to perceive hues as autonomous, absolute colors with their eyes open? Over and over again, and beginning anew with each painting, Geiger attempts to demonstrate pure color, to emancipate color from form and to remove it from context. He has been doing so for more than six decades, and there is probably no other artist on earth who has dealt so intensely with color for so long: "My subject was color and only color from the start."

According to Geiger, his paintings are meant to have the effect of a drum beat, to shock. In the 1950s he experimented with luminous paints and different application techniques in order to energize his colors. In 1952 he was one of the first artists to use special fluorescent paints that appear brighter in daylight than ordinary paints. They give off more visible light than the sunlight falling into the room because they convert the components of daylight invisible to the human eye into longer waves of light. In 1965 Geiger enhanced this effect—which is now commonly seen in advertising—by finely spraying on acrylic paint with a pressure-driven spray gun. The result is a homogeneous, powdery matt surface on which the grains of pigment seem to lie loosely as if sprinkled on. The color seems to float on the surface it has been applied to, shimmering and vibrating. Colored light radiates outward and fills the space between the painting and the viewer. It is as if the color has separated from matter. Although Geiger has never gone as far as James Turrell, who floods entire rooms with ethereal colored light, he too has developed concepts for monochrome spaces. He describes one of his visions as: "A closed spatial capsule, painted bright red inside and illuminated." For a 1975 exhibition in Essen, he built a walk-in cylinder, three meters in diameter, which was spray-painted bright red inside and illuminated with indirect light. His aim was to allow viewers to immerse themselves in color, to soak it up and charge themselves with energy.

Initially there was a great deal of blue in Geiger's paintings, but later on shades of yellow dominated. Since the 1970s he has used the full spectrum of reds: carmine, pink, magenta, vermilion, cadmium red, orange,

1

2

3

4

5

6

4 Neues Rot für Gorbatschow, 1989
Installation at Städtische Galerie im Lenbachhaus, Munich (composed of the works WV 793 and WV 794)
Acrylic, canvas, plaster
355 x 465 x 515 cm

5 Morgen Rot Abend Rot, 2000
Hospital church Heiliggeist, Landshut, Germany
Partial view
Acrylic, canvas
800 x 500 cm
Private collection

6 Berliner Rot II, 2005
Silkscreen with original pigments/BKF Rives, 300 gr, handmade-paper edges
75 x 81 cm, 97 num., sig. Ex. (WVG 224)
Walter Storms Galerie, Munich

Further illustrations:
pp. 28, 86, 120

purple, and reddish violet. "Red is the color, red is beautiful," says Geiger. "Red is life, energy, potency, power, love, warmth and strength. Red gets you high." In addition, red sends the strongest signal and has the greatest luminosity, even though other colors are brighter. To stimulate and enhance the effect of the color in his paintings, Geiger juxtaposes warm and cool shades of red. He also contrasts lighter and darker, and thick and translucent layers. He spray-paints gently ascending gradations of color, which lend his work the illusion of movement and give it an unusual depth. The viewer is able to perceive depth as in a landscape, without forms being used to achieve this effect.

Compared with other types of monochrome or color-field painting, Geiger's works are relatively open to interpretation. Even if their abstraction is emphasized by the often anonymous application of paint, by the synthetic fluorescent paints, and loud, artificial colors like pink, they appear to contain allusions to politics and the natural experiences of sunrise and sunset—to colored phenomena in the atmosphere and the colored light lying over the world, which Geiger experienced as a "war painter" in the Soviet Union and Greece and which he understood as a "spiritual matter." An anecdote he often tells is typical of his relationship with color: shortly after the Second World War, he saw an American girl in a garish red sweater getting into a jeep in bombed-out Munich. The color moved him so deeply that, when he got back to his house, he took the lipstick for his wife out of a CARE package and started to draw a picture in its synthetic, bold color. In 1989 he gave a political title to a spatial installation in the Lenbachhaus in Munich: *New Red for Gorbachev*.

This work consists of a fluorescent pink transverse rectangle in front of a subdued red wall. The rectangle functions as a signal, as a sign of the new spirit of perestroika. Geiger uses only a few elementary forms that do not distract from the color—or, as he explains, that are appropriate to a certain color: the square, the diagonal rectangle, the flattened circle and the transverse oval, partly covered with a sprayed-on aureole. These forms also allude to the sun with its expansive power.

Rupprecht Geiger is an autodidactic painter who has been a loner in the art world throughout his life. In an age when the dominant style was marked by subjective informal gestures, he favored monochromicity and the anonymous application of paint. And he has always remained true to his color-based painting. This is perhaps the reason he is not mentioned in many art histories. Nevertheless, his garishly bright fluorescent paints and his spatial concepts, saturated with light, are of interest to a new generation of artists. Even if there are no direct points of reference, the fluorescent colors in current works by Anselm Reyle and Peter Halley are conspicuous; and Olafur Eliasson's *Weather Project*, the installation of a yellow, circular disk at the Tate Modern in London (October 2003–March 2004), can most definitely be seen as one of Geiger's ideas expanded to infinity.

Text: Markus Zehentbauer

Konstantin Grcic
"Red is an absolute riddle to me"

1 Diana, 2002
Side table
Manufacturer: ClassiCon

2 Vase, 1999
Porcelain vase
Manufacturer: Porzellan Manufaktur Nymphenburg

3 Myto, 2008
Chair
Manufacturer: Plank

4 Chair_One, 2004
Chair
Manufacturer: Magis

5 Odin, 2005
Sofa
Manufacturer: ClassiCon

Munich designer Konstantin Grcic sees color primarily as code. His designs often use the bold colors we know from machines, equipment, and street signs—if they are not black, gray or white. But he's not keen on bright red furniture.

What colors influenced you as a child?
All that occurs to me from my childhood are Lego bricks with their typical colors: Lego red, Lego blue, Lego yellow and Lego gray. The objects I made out of Lego had the same colors. I don't know whether that influenced me or not, but it's an important memory.

But in your designs you do often use these colors.
The colors I use are mostly intense or entirely monochrome. In this case perhaps the colors do have a lot to do with the simplicity of the Lego color palette. I define color nuances in a very intuitive way. My use of color is not subtle but bold and direct.

The use of primary colors could be described as typically German. A good example is the red, yellow, and blue used by Bauhaus designers. Are people still influenced by the country they grow up in as far as colors go?
There is indeed an influence. It was no coincidence that matt black Braun appliances were designed in Germany and the red Olivetti Valentine typewriter in Italy. A person who grows up with the light and the architecture of a Mediterranean country is exposed to entirely different colors than someone who grows up in the north or in Germany. I grew up in Wuppertal, a rather gray town, and gray happens to be one of my favorite colors. But color influences are probably much too complex and subtle to be attributed to countries or childhood experiences. It's also typical that a German artist like Rupprecht Geiger should intensely explore fluorescent colors in an attempt to find a brightness that doesn't exist in Germany. I have two of his simple color fields hanging behind my desk: phosphorescent pink and dark red. I like the monochrome works by Geiger. I love surrounding myself with such things.

Have you ever used fluorescent paints in a design?
I'd love to, but they only have a limited industrial use because they don't keep or are extremely expensive. The things I conjure in my mind are often very colorful, but this intensity of color often disappears on realization of the idea. Color is an important tool in the design process. We use it to mark design elements such as the back or leg of a chair—in the same way others define a color code and mark things with red or yellow. In the early stage of a design, my designs are often very colorful, but then I eliminate the color and make them uniform—it's like dipping them in a bucket of paint. In end products, I find mono-materials and mono-colors the most appealing.

It's the exact opposite for many designers. They develop form without using color and only add it at the end. Is your use of color functional?
For me, color is more schematic. It helps me sort and structure, as in a technical diagram in which colors enable you to see and interpret elements. That's exactly how I use color in the

1
2
3
4
5

6
7
8
9
10

6 Miura, 2005
Bar stool
Manufacturer: Plank

7 Osorom, 2002
Seating element
Manufacturer: Moroso

8 2 Hands, 1996
Laundry basket
Manufacturer: Authentics

9 Pallas, 2003
Table
Manufacturer: ClassiCon

10 Mayday, 1999
Portable lamp
Manufacturer: Flos

Further illustrations:
pp. 195, 211

early stage of a design. At this point it still doesn't have an aesthetic meaning.

So the functional aspects of color don't play a role in the end product?
That's hardly relevant to furniture. I still dream of using color to create modular or multifunctional versions of a design. However, my own highly rational design process tends ultimately to prevent me from pursuing the idea of multifunctionality. In such cases I also prefer to reduce the number of colored versions I have and just keep one or two. Philippe Starck once had a phase in which all his designs were black or gold. That really impressed me. We work for Muji in Japan, and they don't work with color at all. Their color palette consists of nine shades of gray. I find it very exciting to see the colorfulness contained in such a gray scale.

Can your choice of color be described as an aesthetic of machine colors?
Yes, that's an apt description of my design process, which is like creating a diagram of how something works. Color is also used as a code for machines. In this case color has credibility and doesn't need to offer an emotive argument to buy the product. There is interaction between form and color, but form is clearly dominant.

Would you prefer each design to be produced in only one particular color?
I've recently had a number of talks with manufacturers about the illusion that a design can be sold in a large number of colors. Sure, you can use color to change things, but that's taking the easy approach. A red chair looks different from a black chair, but is the red color as effective? If I had my way, I would offer every form in just a single color.

Chair_One, for example, just in black?
Chair_One is what inspired this idea. We first made it in just dark gray, red, and white, and only afterward in black. The black version is the most powerful. If I had my way, I'd withdraw the other versions from the market. I'd also prefer only a black version of the Magis 360° stool, but it's sold in orange, olive green, and blue as well. These colors are good examples of the machine aesthetic. They come from a functional context, from the military, or from a professional environment.

Do you think it's problematic to adapt older designs to changed tastes using color?
No, it can even be exciting. For me color is an interchangeable code.

Do some designs sell especially well in a color that you see as less than perfect?
Yes, manufacturers always claim that they definitely need a piece of furniture in the black, white, and red colors you see in all office furniture catalogues. And that's precisely the order in which they sell best. But these three colors, together, are really ugly. And red is a very difficult color for a piece of furniture. For the Miura stool, for example, we selected curry yellow and an almost brownish oxide red, which suited the design, but didn't sell. The manufacturer, Plank, has nevertheless kept these colors for the product line. The photos that have been published in the press usually show the stool in these colors, but when people go to the store, they buy it in black, white, or bright red. This kind of red is an absolute riddle to me as a choice of color for a piece of furniture. But as long as the color that's important to me is included in the line, I don't try to fight it. I have preferences, but there is no color that I absolutely hate.

Interview: Markus Frenzl

UNStudio
The Digital Glow

1 La Defense, Almere, The Netherlands, 2004
Office complex

2 Circle, 2005
Sofa
Manufacturer: Walter Knoll

3 MUMUTH Music Theater, Graz, Austria, 2008

With its spectacular architecture such as the Möbius House, the Mercedes-Benz-Museum and the Erasmus Bridge, UNStudio ("united net for architecture, urbanism and infrastructure") has become closely associated with the type of acceleration and vitalization of architecture that can be achieved using computers. The firm's two founders, Ben van Berkel and Caroline Bos, are both digital designers who work not only with free-form shapes but also networked planning and construction—and a new understanding of color. For them color is at once a display element and an orientation mark, a statement, and a digital signature.

Their colors seem to have originated from a digital palette; it is almost as if their surfaces and facades have been directly imported from a computer or are themselves fluctuating animations. One spectacular example is the iridescent Galleria Department Store in Seoul, which was opened in 2004. Here, 4,330 glass discs and a special iridescent lamina cause light to be refracted across the facade; by night this nacreous effect is replaced by LED animations. Like a facetted insect eye, the outside surface fluoresces and dances, seeming almost about to dissolve. A similarly dynamic effect is achieved by the pulsating media facade of the Star Place shopping center in Kaohsiung (2008), where ever-changing waves of color unobtrusively direct the observer to the escalators. The artificial becomes the real; we no longer see the surface color but instead the immaterial color orchestrated using lighting technology.

An apparently more solid example is the Agora Theater in the Dutch city of Lelystad (2007). Here, angled surfaces in red, ocher, and orange correspond to the building's interior free-form spaces. The building envelope has a topographic character; color variations and the tin facade create a folded structure, a piece of origami that takes up the aesthetic of a stealth bomber and transforms it into a cultural beacon. The building's core, a blood-red auditorium, and the violet stairway sculpture that swings through the space are the key elements in the architects' color-coding of the building's individual sections, creating an effect like a CAD rendering that has accidentally developed into a three-dimensional form. They have allowed floors, walls, and ceilings to flow into one another or interlaced forms and colors to generate hybrids, chimeras of the digital age.

The UNStudio architects consistently break with conventional perceptions of not only material and forms but also colors. This is impressively illustrated by the La Defense office complex in Almere (2004). The jagged, serpentine structure is equipped with a special glass facade exhibiting a color palette that alternates between yellow, red, blue, and violet depending on where you are standing. The courtyard forms the crystallization point of a color design involving carefully calculated tonal interplays generated by a special foil integrated into the glass surfaces.

"Organization is the most important aspect," says van Berkel, whereas form is the "last stage of the process—the most insignificant aspect." He no longer thinks in terms of singulars but in terms of series. Once solutions have been found they can be fused and further developed at any time, and a solution is always part of a

1

2

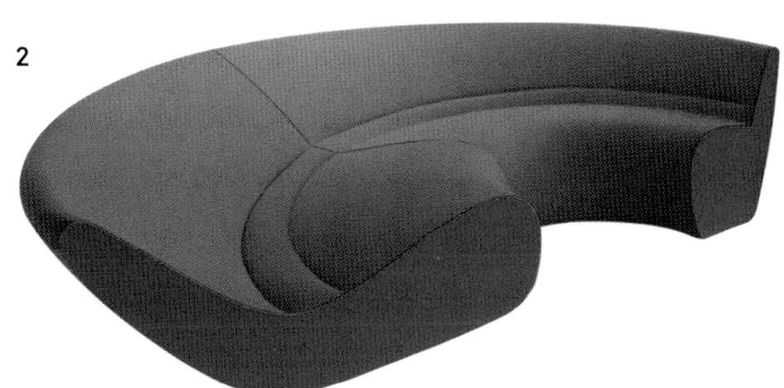

3

4

5

6

7

4 VilLA NM, Upstate New York, USA, 2007
Private residence

5 MYchair, 2008
Armchair
Manufacturer: Walter Knoll

6 Galleria, Seoul, South Korea, 2004
Department store

7 Star Place, Kaohsiung, Taiwan, 2008
Facade design for a shopping center

Further illustrations: pp. 54, 71

developmental trajectory. Van Berkel favors the idea over the form, the matrix over the material, and the flow over the final product. This is evident, for instance, in the Research Laboratory completed in 2008 at the University of Groningen, which features an atrium resembling a flamethrower. Pale yellow at the base, the heat ray weakens in intensity as it moves upwards, deepening to orange and finally red. With its helix stairway, this new building positioned between the University Hospital and the Medical Faculty seems to be wrapped around its two vertical interior voids. The surface of the facade is formed by a rhombic net of aluminum slats, the inner sides of which have a yellow-green color. On the lower level of the building yellow predominates and is gradually replaced by green towards the top of the building, which references the neighboring park.

Anyone suggesting boundlessness also emphasizes breaks, edges, and segments. The individual segments of the sofa Circle appear to be cut through as if by a hot wire. And in the case of the voluminous MYchair, which UNStudio also designed for Walter Knoll, the cross-sectional surfaces are accentuated by gaudy colors. Contrasting yellow-green and anthracite bite into one another, a contrast reflected in the juxtaposition of the projecting cushion with its play of concave and convex forms and the seemingly fragile base made of metal tubing. Here we find a case of color shaping form. This is the big difference between MYchair and the architecture that seeks a high light density yet blurs surfaces and dissipates building elements with changing digital colors. Its color spectrum stems from the computer itself—absolutely artificial and constantly in flux. The UNStudio approach thus runs counter to the traditional architectural attitude that tends to emphasize the material's own color. Colors glow autonomously from within, materials fluctuate, and facades dance.

Text: Oliver Herwig

Gerhard Richter
Ways of Seeing

1 Color Fields. 6 Arrangements of 1260 Colors: a (yellow-red-blue), 1974
Offset print on white cardboard
Each 64.4 x 79.2 cm
Olbricht Collection, Essen
(GR Ed. 51, Ex. 17/32)
© Gerhard Richter

2 25 Farben (25 Colors), 2007
Lacquer on Alu-Dibond
48.5 x 48.5 cm
Private collection
(GR 902-50)
© Gerhard Richter

3 Southern Transept Window, 2007
Cologne Cathedral
© Gerhard Richter, Cologne/ Dombauarchiv Cologne, Matz and Schenk

In the 1980s, Gerhard Richter was regarded as the "chameleon of German art." The heterogeneous character of his work was either criticized as amounting to a succession of stylistic incongruities or admired as fascinatingly radical. The possibility of this work being informed by a consistent outlook was something that did not even occur to most observers. For how could someone produce blurred paintings based on amateur photographs and find urban landscapes and romantic seascapes as worthy of portrayal as photos from newspaper reports such as those used for *Eight Student Nurses* (1966)? How could someone literally "exhibit" colors in serial color charts and simply call the result *1025 Colors* (1974)? How could someone produce gray canvases, family portraits, flower still lifes, and abstract paintings?

It took some time for the insight to emerge that what seemed so arbitrary was in fact not really arbitrary at all. Today it has long been clear that Richter's work is unified by a directed indifference to a consistent pictorial method and his role as an observer and filter of contemporary pictorial culture. At the beginning of the 1960s, Richter's visual horizon comprised mainly black and white TV and newspaper images, and family photos. Later the inclusion of color photography brought with it new subjects and photographic points of view. Richter's inventory of contemporary visual culture is manifested particularly clearly in his encyclopedic *Atlas* project, which he has been pursuing since 1962. This work, which Richter first exhibited in 1997 at Documenta X in Kassel, combines sketches and photos by the artist with other photos and newspaper cuttings. Referring to his use of press and amateur photography, Richter claimed that for him such photos had "no style, no composition, no judgment; it liberated me from personal experience. There was nothing, but a pure picture."(1)

In his color charts, the attitude of indifference is combined with pure seeing. Richter produced the first of these pictures in 1966, modeling them on the color sample cards used by house painters. Here, Richter reduces the image to the factual, consciously somewhat laconically manifested presence of color. In contrast to his work drawing on photography, the model here is not motif-based but material and conveyed via the direct application of standardized colors. Image and subject thus become one. Initially Richter varied the sequence of templates arbitrarily, as seen in the case of *Six Colors* or *Eighteen Colors* (both 1966). However, from 1971 onwards he begins to more clearly objectify his deployment of color and to disconnect it from the reference to sample cards. He now calculates the number of fields according to mixtures of the primary colors red, yellow, and blue. A twofold mixture, for instance, produces twelve tones (3 x 2 x 2), their sevenfold refraction according to light/dark a further 168—thus in total *180 Colors* (1971). In a subsequent phase Richter develops his division schema from three primary colors plus gray (later green) in multiplicative four-step stages. The result is charts comprising 4, 16, 64, 256 and 1,024 fields respectively, in which he mixes the basic tones equally and distributes them randomly. Richter now gauges the size of the individual fields in proportion with the overall size in

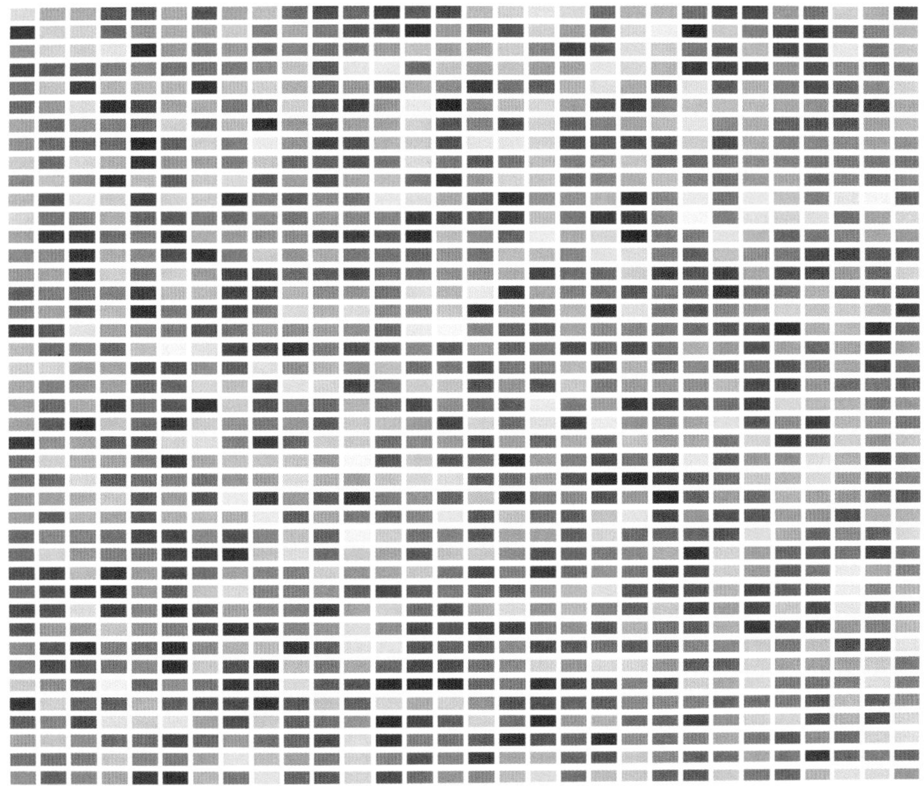

1

2

3

5

4

6

4 4096 Farben
(4096 Colors), 1974
Lacquer on canvas
254 x 254 cm
(GR 359)

5 Grau (Gray), 1974
Oil on canvas
200 x 150 cm
Kunstmuseum Bonn
(GR 366-3)

6 Achtzehn Farben (Eighteen Colors), 1966/1992
Lacquer on Alucobond
18 panels, each 28 x 130 cm, overall dimension 240 x 450 cm
Frieder Burda Collection
(GR 140)

Further illustrations:
pp. 200, 229, 249

order to concentrate the color even more and to increase its objective character. A group work from 1974 is probably the most consistent example of Richter integrating his approach to color fields in terms of formal processes, proportions and pictorial logic. Beginning with the 20 by 20 centimeter *4 Colors* (1974) —consisting of primary colors plus green— the format increases progressively in parallel with the complexity of the paint mixtures until it reaches the 299 by 299 centimeter *1024 Colors* (1974). The series shows a leap from quantity to quality. The increasing complexity of the mixtures and degree of proliferation gives rise to a potentially infinite divisibility and abundance, which lends the color greater presence. The additive formalization of the means—Richter's "indifference"—evolves into an enhanced pictorial impression. Indeed, for Richter this objectivity is a means to let the "color have its effect in all its brilliance and richness."(2)

The idea of an "objective" efficacy of color can be traced from Richter's early color charts via the color permutations seen for instance in *4096 Colors* (1974), to the *Southern Transept Window* (2007) for the Cologne Cathedral. Richter designed the 113 square meter window for the facade of the southern transept incorporating a total of 11,263 square elements with an edge length of 9.6 centimeters. The idea behind the design can be traced back to *4096 Colors*. In order to achieve the greatest possible tonal variation, Richter used a random generator to establish the order of colors. The results were then further refined to remove any regular patterns. In this case, Richter reduced the color scope found in his painting to mixtures of only 72 colors. On the one hand, this limitation was a response to the fact that the elements were to be made from glass produced using antique methods. On the other hand, it was also based on conceptual reasons. When paint is used on canvas, the number of tones is fixed once the colors have been mixed. However, in the case of a stained-glass window, sunlight—which is constantly changing—assumes the role of the color white, and subjects the material to endless modulation. What Richter calls the "brilliance and richness of color," is thus directly visible—unemotional yet celebratory.

Richter's monochromatic gray painting represents an antipole to this work. He has said that around 1968 he sometimes painted canvases gray when he didn't know, "what there was to paint."(3) He subsequently saw that the neutrality of gray was particularly appropriate to "demonstrate 'nothing'."(4) These pictures are extreme examples of a non-representation that is barely perceivable as painting. Here, Richter undertakes a detailed exploration of what constitutes neutrality in painting. The pictures exhibit different, usually medium-range nuances of gray and are characterized by both a gestural and mechanical approach to structuring. The surfaces are sometimes regular, sometimes abruptly structured by brushstrokes, sometimes evenly rolled, dabbed with sponges, or evenly smeared over. Richter himself once described gray as "the welcome and only possible way of expressing indifference, the refusal to make a statement, a lack of opinion, and a lack of form."(5) This group of works sees the artist entering a liminal zone: in excluding color he undertakes to demonstrate non-representation. Given these parameters, the multiplicity of resulting works is all the more astonishing. They include gray paintings that seem almost to be landscapes, works with a pronounced material character, and large, uniform monochromes that generate the impression of comprehensive neutrality from the soft, barely perceptible visual vibration of a shade of gray. As in all Richter's work, even in the particular case of such indifferent pictures, it is always the painting that leads to a specific form of perception—thus transforming the work into sensory experience.

Text: Jens Asthoff

(1) Gerhard Richter, "Interview mit Rolf Schön," in *36. Biennale von Venedig* [Cat.], 1972, pp. 23–25.
(2) Gerhard Richter, in *Planned Painting* [Cat.], Palais des Beaux-Arts, Brussels, 1974.
(3) Gerhard Richter, in *Fundamental Painting* [Cat.], Stedelijk Museum, Amsterdam, 1975.
(4) Ibid.
(5) Ibid.

Ronan & Erwan Bouroullec
"Color is like a skin"

1 Vegetal, 2008
Chair
Manufacturer: Vitra

2 Butterfly, 2002
Shelf
Manufacturer: Cappellini

3 Clouds, 2008
Assembling system made of textile modules
Manufacturer: Kvadrat

4 Rocs, 2006
Partition elements
Manufacturer: Vitra

Given the choice, French designers Ronan and Erwan Bouroullec prefer to design objects that don't steal the show. Subdued colors with gradated shades of gray dominate the color palette of their furniture and objects—even though consumers usually favor black, white, and red over shades of brown and green.

What role do colors play in your designs?
It's changed over time. When we started out, we used the natural colors of the materials without adding anything else. For example, we used untreated wood for wooden furniture. White also predominated because it is the "natural" color of a variety of synthetic materials such as Corian and polystyrene and also the color of plain ceramic. At some point we began experimenting with variations of selected colors such as blue, green, brown, and gray.

Your designs today often incorporate colors that are familiar from the natural world.
What we have taken from nature is perhaps the idea of color diversity and modulation. There are never monochrome, pure colors in nature. The colors are variegated and constantly changing. But it is true that we use colors that seem natural: variations of blue, green, and brown. So even if it is not a conscious process, we probably have natural colors in mind when we make our choices on the color fan.

Are there other sources of inspiration for colors? An artist or the color palette of a specific era, perhaps?
Not really. We take an intuitive rather than an analytical approach to color. We don't draw on other artists' color concepts, although they're naturally of interest to us. We're deeply moved, for instance, by the way Donald Judd works with color.

What color systems do you work with?
We use the NCS, which has the most comprehensive color fans available. Sometimes we also use fans for special materials, such as plastics. It depends on the material we want to use.

Is there a color concept that underlies all your designs?
No, it always depends on the project in question. When it comes to certain colors, it would perhaps be most fitting to talk about "scales." We seldom use saturated colors but instead try to take a subtle approach to certain shades and to avoid loud colors. We usually end up with colored shades of gray.

At what point in the design process does color come into play?
Always at the end. Otherwise it would only distract from the central idea of the project, from its form, function, and technology.

Do you pick out the color of the manufactured versions of your designs?
We make the decision ourselves of course, but there are times when we also discuss the issue with the company. For example, for the selection of colors for the Vegetal chair, we held talks with Hella Jongerius, who developed a new concept for Vitra. But it was all very informal. When it comes to color, there are hardly any rational arguments. It's much more about sharing perceptions.

2

1

3

4

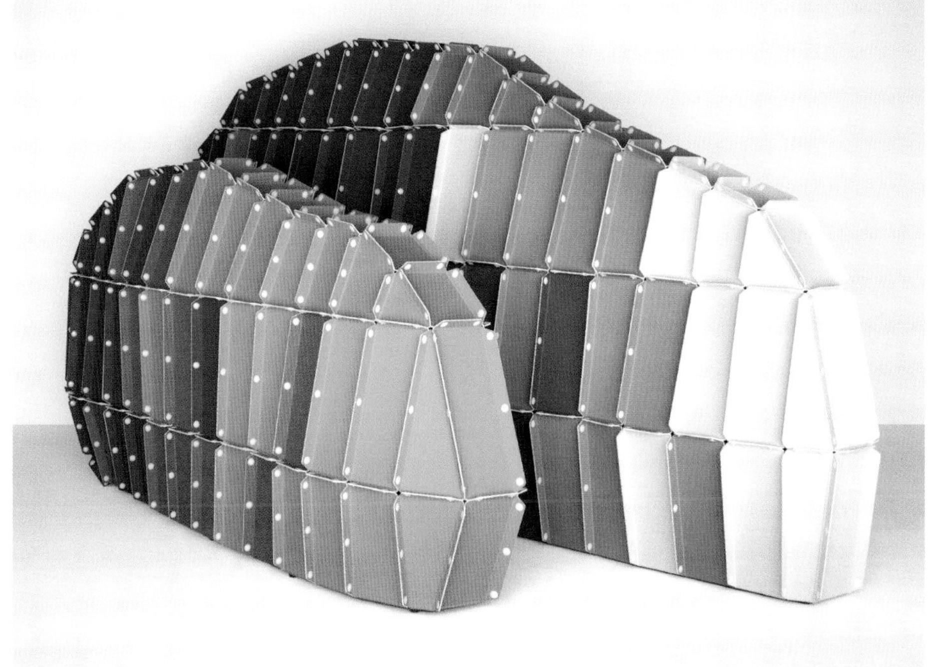

5

6

7

8

5 North Tiles, Kvadrat showroom, Stockholm, 2006
Assembling system made of textile modules
Manufacturer: Kvadrat

6 Centerpiece, 2001
Colored object
Manufacturer: Coromandel

7 Vase, 2001
Light object
Manufacturer: Galerie Kreo, Paris

8 Assemblage, 2004
5-piece installation
Manufacturer: Galerie Kreo, Paris

Further illustrations:
pp. 67, 84

Are there any colors you would never use?
There are no colors that we're afraid of, but there are indeed colors that we never use. This isn't because we consider them wrong, but because they don't fit in with our projects or the atmosphere we want to create. Pink and yellow are great colors, but they haven't suited any of our projects yet.

Are there functional aspects that you try to communicate through color?
It's not directly a question of function. However, if you believe that the main function of a sofa is to look and be comfortable, color selection is very important. That's why we prefer mellow colors for such inviting pieces of furniture. Colors can somehow cause the release of pheromones in the body and so arouse feelings. Some colors stand for comfort, softness, tranquility, and harmony. And since we try to create objects that are not too loud and that meet the demands placed on them, a subtle choice of colors is often essential. This thought was the starting point for our Clouds modular textile system, which we designed for Kvadrat. The colors needed to ensure that the elements made out of the Clouds could be easily integrated into home interiors, like vegetable entities. The various nuances of color give the Clouds depth, particularly when these color nuances are not perfectly coordinated.

Are there customer color preferences that have surprised you? Do certain colors sell well?
Of course there are some colors that sell better than others, but we try not to let them influence us, and we continue to use shades of green even though they don't sell well because we have a deep conviction that they are honest colors that suit our projects.

Is it possible to refresh an older design by using contemporary colors? Or should the color of a product become a permanent symbol of the period in which it was designed?
Projects are bound to evolve, and we don't have any objection to renewing projects by adapting their colors. Color is like a skin.

Interview: Markus Frenzl

Anselm Reyle
"What I look for first is dissonance"

1 Untitled, 2007
Acrylic paint
(variable dimensions)
Solo exhibiton: Installation view "Construction of Harmony," Galerie Almine Rech, Paris, 2007

Courtesy of Almine Rech Gallery Brussels/Paris

2 Untitled, 2006
Mixed media on canvas
224 x 189 cm
Private collection

Courtesy of Andersen's Contemporary Copenhagen/Berlin and Nicolai Frahm, London/ Basel

3 Untitled, 2007
Mixed media on canvas, acrylic glass
143 x 121 x 18.5 cm
Private collection

Courtesy of Almine Rech Gallery Brussels/Paris

Anselm Reyle combines materials and colors that are usually frowned upon in art circles. In his paintings and sculptures he uses glittering car paint, cheap glossy foil, and neon colors. He thereby tests the boundaries of what is considered aesthetically acceptable, not only to provoke but also to illuminate our cultural taboos and the allure they have.

Are there any modernist artists who have influenced your approach to color?
Above all I would say that Cézanne has been important to my work. I'm interested in his segmentation of clearly differentiated blocks of color. A modified form of this approach can also be seen in the work of Otto Freundlich. I was still young when my parents started taking me to galleries. I remember spotting a painting by Freundlich twenty meters away and feeling it trigger something emotional in me. As a rule, abstract art doesn't appeal to children. A painting by Blinky Palermo had a similar effect on me, although at the time I was unable to understand it on an intellectual level. My own work is in part also concerned with the very direct effect of color. A picture should communicate something without the viewer requiring any particular knowledge.

How do you plan your paintings?
I have a shelf full of sample colors and materials that I use to investigate different effects. Someone had the idea that I should test the colors before applying them to canvas so that I wouldn't have to throw so much away. So I started painting strips of cardboard in different colors and laying them next to one another to try out color combinations. I began planning and constructing paintings and later I also began having some produced.

You now employ up to thirty staff members in your studio. What effect has this had on the quantity and quality of your paintings?
That was an important step for my work and has made it more conceptual. Because I produce paintings relatively quickly in comparison to other artists, I don't find it very difficult to discard a painting that I'm not satisfied with. In the case of my gestural paintings, up to 90 percent of them come to nothing. By working with assistants I gain a distance from my work that perhaps allows me to judge it more honestly and objectively.

What effect do you aim for? What are the criteria that inform your color combinations?
Usually I first consider which colors are totally incompatible. For example, I might take an orange and juxtapose it with a neon orange. The result is an orange that seems almost brownish and doesn't really have a chance. The material also plays a role. A violet applied to a reflective surface as a glaze acquires a chrome gloss and has a completely different effect, for instance, to a matt, water-based paint in an identical color. These differences produce highly varied effects and thus make very different statements.

Would it be right to say that you're more interested in friction than harmony?
Harmony is something I usually arrive at automatically. What I look for first is dissonance. Earlier, when I was making decisions about

1

2

3

4

5

6

7

4 Untitled, 2006
Mixed media on canvas, acrylic glass
234 x 199 x 20 cm
Private collection

Courtesy of Gavin Brown's enterprise

5 Untitled, 2009
Mixed media on canvas, stainless steel frame
135 x 114 cm

Courtesy of Almine Rech Gallery Brussels/Paris

6 Harmony, 2008
Bronze, effect lacquer, plinth with macassar wood veneer
90 x 90 x 40 cm

Courtesy of Almine Rech Gallery Brussels/Paris

7 Untitled, 2006
Acrylic on canvas
285 x 625 cm
Private collection

Courtesy of Almine Rech Gallery Brussels/Paris

Further illustrations: pp. 88, 151, 199, 270

color composition while actually painting, this process was more impulsive—although I have never really trusted the idea that creative and artistic work "brings the innermost to the surface." For this reason alone, I've always enjoyed using colors with which I've had a distant relationship. For example, I used to find lilac dreadful, but now it is one of my favorite colors.

Why do you use neon colors?
I've had direct experience with the way LSD alters perception and heightens colors. The psychedelic aesthetic of the 1970s is one of the influences on my art. In the 1980s neon was also a part of punk—for instance, on record covers—and was used to signal an aggressive, "anti" attitude. When I used neon colors at the art academy, I was told: "You have to generate light by other means." Neon was regarded as somehow unfair. Breaking such rules has become part of my work.

What is it about gestural painting that's still interesting today?
What interests and fascinates me is the questionable claim of these paintings to be serious art: three blobs of paint smeared on the canvas and that's it! Exploring this dubious claim is the basis of my work. It's important to me that each work simultaneously says that it is merely three stupid blobs or stupid stripes.

Are your works ironic commentaries on art?
I see it more in terms of distance. It's about more than irony. I want to offer an alternative to pure negation, which isn't easy. For instance, I can never say what is good or bad taste. I was raised with an awareness of "good" taste only to find that I was more interested in what was purportedly "bad" taste. So that was what I preferred to focus on. Many of my combinations of materials are regarded as "trashy" and tend to be dismissed as "merely decorative" or "sensationalist." I consciously work with elements that tend to be frowned upon in so-called high art circles.

Nevertheless, you are excited by the culturally worthless. For instance, you make bronze sculptures based on soapstone figurines and coat them with a glittering car paint.
That's a good example of aesthetic and cultural taboos, and it certainly also has to do with irony. These forms and surfaces interest me because I know that in their original context they're regarded by the art public as completely alien to art. On the one hand, you have a type of African handicraft that doesn't have a long tradition at all. This type of soapstone sculpture has only been produced over the last sixty years. On the other hand, I can produce a version of this sculpture that is considered worthy of being exhibited in a gallery. Even paint from the car-tuning industry appears surprisingly meaningful in this context.

What effect does this so-called Scarab paint have?
It has a large color spectrum and shimmers in different colors, such as green or violet, depending on the angle of view. Using it in a completely different context also has a purely formal significance, since the effect is better on these rounded sculptures than, for example, on a Golf GTI.

Are there times when you lose control of the dynamic between the colors?
Occurrences of the unexpected are very important moments because they generate elements that can subsequently be deployed quite deliberately. I accidentally dripped paint on one of my first stripe paintings. I liked the effect because it fractured the strict dogma of pure formalism, which I don't believe in anyway. The blots also proved to be a positive addition to the composition. I subsequently fleshed out the blots—with a rim like an accidental imprint from a paint tin and a drop that had dribbled downwards. Since then I've often used blots in my stripe paintings.They've become a kind of signature.

Interview: Silke Hohmann

Biographies and Brief Profiles

A

David Adjaye
267
David Adjaye (b. 1966) is one of the most renowned young British architects of his generation. The son of Ghanaian parents, Adjaye grew up in Cairo and Saudi Arabia and later studied at London's Middlesex and South Bank universities and at the Royal College of Art. In 1994 he founded the firm of Adjaye & Russell with William Russell, and in 2000 he established Adjaye Associates. His most important projects, such as the Bernie Grant Arts Centre in Tottenham, have been built in the UK and America. He also collaborates with artists such as Chris Ofili and Olafur Eliasson. Working in consultation with graphic designer Peter Saville, Adjaye designed the London showroom for the Danish textile manufacturer Kvadrat, which includes an elongated central stairway accentuated with walls of tinted glass that reflect a rainbow spectrum of colors.
www.adjaye.com

ahrens grabenhorst architekten
99
Roger Ahrens (b. 1963) and Gesche Grabenhorst (b. 1962) established their architectural practice in Berlin in 1995 but have since relocated to Hanover. Ahrens previously studied at the Braunschweig University of Technology, the Swiss Federal Institute of Technology Lausanne, and the Berlin University of Technology; Grabenhorst studied at the Munich University of Technology and the Braunschweig University of Art, and since 2006 she has held a professorship at the University of Bielefeld. The most well-known projects undertaken by the two architects include the remodeling of a church into the community center of the Hanover Liberal Jewish Community (2009) and the extension of the Celle Art Museum (2006)—a cube with a glass facade backlit with computer-controlled LED batten lighting. By night the 1,272 diodes emit white light that is interrupted hourly by short loops featuring seamless transitions from yellow to green to blue and from orange to red to violet.
www.ahrensgrabenhorst.de

Shay Alkalay
50, 146
Shay Alkalay (b. 1976) and his wife, Yael Mer (b. 1976), founded the London design studio Raw-Edges in 2007. The two Israelis met while studying at the Bezalel Academy of Art and Design in Jerusalem and both continued their studies at the Royal College of Art in London. They experiment with materials such as felt and Tyvek, as well as with different furniture typologies. For the London design firm Established & Sons, Alkalay designed, under his own name, the Stack chest of drawers, which has no exterior frame. Instead, the individual drawers are stacked on top of each other to create a sculptural, multi-colored object.
www.raw-edges.com

Allford Hall Monaghan Morris Architects
20
Simon Allford (b. 1961), Jonathan Hall (b. 1960), Paul Monaghan (b. 1962), and Peter Morris (b. 1962) founded their own architectural firm in London in 1989 and now employ more than a hundred people. Their best-known projects include the new Saatchi Gallery, for which they redesigned a classicist building in London; the refurbished Barbican Arts Centre in London, built in the Brutalist style; and the two striking Unity Liverpool towers on the Liverpudlian waterfront. The architects often use color to structure large surfaces or to provide better orientation. Finely gradated shades seem to dissolve into color blends in such projects as the Adelaide Wharf apartment building and the Westminster Academy in London, as well as the Barking Central complex in Essex.
www.ahmm.co.uk

Ron Arad
106, 178
Born in Tel Aviv in 1951 and now based in London, Ron Arad moves effortlessly between the fields of design, architecture, and art. After studying at the Bezalel Academy of Arts and Design in Jerusalem and the Architectural Association School of Architecture (AA) in London, he founded the design studio One Off in London with Caroline Thormann, which functioned both as a workshop and a showroom. His first design, the Rover Chair, which he built himself from an old car seat and steel piping, has long been recognized as a design classic. Today Arad designs voluptuous pieces of furniture that are produced in limited editions from highly polished aluminum or Corian, as well as variations for mass production. His clients include Vitra, Kartell, Moroso, Driade, Alessi, and Magis. In 2008/09 a spectacular retrospective of his work was shown at the Centre Pompidou in Paris and at New York's MoMA.
www.ronarad.com

B

Maarten Baas
18, 116, 176, 191
Dutch designer Maarten Baas (b. 1978) studied at the Design Academy Eindhoven and today has a studio in 's-Hertogenbosch. In 2006 he presented the handcrafted furniture series Clay at the Milan Furniture Fair. This cheerful collection is made of clay and metal and, with its colors and forms recalling play dough, it alludes to the anonymity of mass production.
www.maartenbaas.com

John Baldessari
14, 64, 104, 241, 272
John Baldessari (b. 1931) is an American conceptual artist. From 1949 to 1959 he studied at five different Californian universities and in the late sixties began producing works that combined pictorial material from the mass media with texts, often creating an absurd effect, for instance, by juxtaposing images with quotations from art critics or books on art. His work represents a play between signs and their meaning that can be traced back to the structuralist and poststructuralist theories that Baldessari was interested in at the time. He later painted over faces in photographs with shiny monochrome colors, thus denying the beholder a view of the essential. He designed a color code for these blank spaces, which further multiplied the ambiguity of his images. Baldessari took part in Documenta 5 and 7. He lives in Santa Monica in California, and in 2009 was awarded the Golden Lion by the Venice Biennale for his life's work.
www.baldessari.org

BarberOsgerby
81, 124, 131, 136, 164, 168, 197
Edward Barber (b. 1969) and Jay Osgerby (b. 1969) met while they were studying architecture at the Royal College of Art in London. In 1996 they opened an office in the city and since then have been designing predominantly furniture for brands such as Cappellini, Magis, Authentics, Venini, and Established & Sons. Their designs appear to be based on simple ideas but are refined down to the last detail. BarberOsgerby have a particular interest in surfaces and colors and their work is characterized by tonal harmonies, transparencies, and overlays. The tables in their "Iris" series refer directly to the tonalities found in color fans. Each aluminum table features several shades of one color, which are applied using an electrolytic process, resulting in an unusual, iridescent surface.
www.barberosgerby.com

Baumschlager Eberle
117
Carlo Baumschlager (b. 1956) and Dietmar Eberle (b. 1952) opened their architectural office in Lochau near Bregenz in Austria in 1985. Housing estates and energy conservation are central aspects of their work.

They now have a staff of over 100 working for them in seven locations, including Beijing and Hong Kong. In 2008 their design was realized for the so-called Nordwesthaus, near their headquarters in Fussach. This building takes the form of a giant cube with a constantly changing appearance, towering out of Lake Constance. The concrete bearing walls inside with their biomorphic apertures contrast interestingly with an exterior envelope covered in a crystalline pattern. Behind the glass facade 1,500 individually-controlled LEDs allow the building to be illuminated in an enormous range of colors.
www.baumschlager-eberle.com

Jurgen Bey
173, 217
Rotterdam resident Jurgen Bey (b. 1965) regards himself more as a researcher than as a designer of finished products; he makes design about design. Trained at the Design Academy Eindhoven, he now teaches at the Royal College of Art in London. One of his most well-known designs is the Tree Trunk Bench (1999) for Droog Design, but he has also covered historical and everyday pieces of furniture with an elastic skin or rough rope and built furniture from wooden transport crates. Since 2002 he has run Studio Makkink & Bey with his wife, the architect Rianna Makkink (b. 1964). In 2006, with the help of an investor, they founded the office-furniture firm Prooff, which stands for "progressive office."
www.jurgenbey.nl

BLESS
39, 193–194, 243
The Austrian Désirée Heiss (b. 1971), who works in Paris, and the German Ines Kaag (b. 1970), who has her own studio in Berlin, have been running the BLESS fashion label since 1997. Both women studied fashion design, Heiss with Vivienne Westwood at the University of Applied Arts in Vienna, and Kaag at the University of Applied Sciences in Hanover. The BLESS designers create clothes, objects, and furniture that combine elements from the worlds of fashion, art, architecture, and design. Moreover, they employ unusual materials in unusual combinations to serve unusual functions, one example being the ordinary computer cable they transformed into jewelry by threading it with gilded plastic beads.
www.bless-service.de

Mattia Bonetti
42, 101, 159
Mattia Bonetti was born in 1952 in Lugano, where he studied industrial design before moving to Paris in 1973. In 1978 he designed the furnishings for the nightclub Le Palace, and in 1981 presented his first furniture collection in cooperation with Elisabeth Garouste. The two went on to develop a brand identity for Christian Lacroix. Other examples of their work include packaging for Shiseido and Nina Ricci. Since 2002 Bonetti has been working alone, creating above all furnishings for galleries such as David Gill in London. His latest work includes a collection of occasional furnishings and tables made of fiberglass and coated with a metallic lacquer. Depending on the angle of view and the incidence of light, the surfaces of these pieces fluoresce with different colors, changing, for instance, from metallic violet to metallic green.
www.davidgillgalleries.com

Astrid Bornheim Architektur
224–225
Berlin architect Astrid Bornheim (b. 1968) studied at the Braunschweig University of Technology and at Vienna's University of Technology and University of Applied Arts. She opened her own office in 2003, specializing in enterprise and exhibition architecture. Her projects have included the Weissenhof gallery in Stuttgart and the Centre of German Architecture (DAZ) in Berlin. Bornheim has also developed a facade for the headquarters of the firm Eternit in Heidelberg, a building designed in 1964 by Ernst Neufert. The facade, which was designed to complement the firm's brand, features lesenes (facings and structural elements) set at different angles in the corporate colors of green and red. These add accents to the exterior, which is otherwise dominated by large fiber-cement panels.
www.astridbornheim.de

Ayzit Bostan
134
The Munich fashion designer Ayzit Bostan was born in Turkey in 1968 and arrived in Germany with her family at the age of four. After a tailor's apprenticeship she went on to study at the German Master School for Fashion in Munich and presented her first collection in 1995. Bostan designs minimalist pieces from monochromatic fabrics but adds sophisticated details that are often only apparent on closer inspection. Since 2008 the independent fashion designer has also been working for the leather goods manufacturer Bree, producing a handbag collection that is constantly expanding.
www.ayzitbostan.de

Ronan & Erwan Bouroullec
67, 84, 300–303
The brothers Ronan (b. 1971) and Erwan (b. 1976) Bouroullec grew up in Brittany. They have been working together in Paris since 1997, when they were discovered by Giulio Cappellini at the Paris Furniture Fair. Both of them studied design, Ronan at the École Nationale Supérieure des Arts Décoratifs (ENSAD) in Paris, and Erwan at the École Nationale Supérieure d'Arts in the Parisian suburb of Cergy. Today their clients include brands such as Cappellini, Ligne Roset, Vitra, Magis, and Kvadrat. The brothers design furniture and spatial objects, deriving their structures from nature. This also applies to their colors, which often include green and brown tones.
www.bouroullec.com

Fernando Brízio
244
For Fernando Brízio (b. 1968) design is about the presentation of a process. Some years ago the Portuguese designer drove a jeep in wavy lines until the pre-fired ceramic vessels in the boot succumbed to gravity and warped. For a recent series he mounted a number of felt-tip pens on a white ceramic vase and let the colors slowly run out. After a time individual spots of color formed and then ran together and blended. The project, entitled *Painting with Giotto*, was exhibited by the Kreo gallery in Paris. Other clients of Brízio's include Droog Design, Fabrica, and Cor Unum. He lives in Lisbon and is a professor at the ESAD College of Art and Design near Caldas da Rainha.
www.fernandobrizio.com

C

Fernando & Humberto Campana
123, 276–279
The most successful designers in Latin America today did not take the most direct route to their profession. Humberto Campana (b. 1953) studied law in Rio Clara and then tried his hand as an artist. His brother, Fernando (b. 1961), completed an architecture degree in São Paulo, where the two founded a design studio in 1983. However, it was not until the late nineties that the Campana brothers first achieved recognition, when the Italian manufacturer edra started to manufacture their experimental furniture designs. The Campanas often use found materials such as stuffed animals, string, and strips of leather.
www.campanas.com.br

Maarten De Ceulaer
139
Maarten De Ceulaer (b. 1983) lives in Brussels and studied interior design there at St. Lukas Hogeschool, and product design at the Design Academy Eindhoven. His graduating project, *A Pile of Suitcases*, was produced in a limited edition by the Nilufar gallery in Milan and is now manufactured by the Italian firm Casamania in an altered form. The assemblage of six leather suitcases in different tones of green constitutes a flexible cupboard. The suitcases are linked at the back and can be combined in different arrangements.
www.maartendeceulaer.com

Pierre Charpin
63, 97, 132, 138
Pierre Charpin (b. 1962) only began designing furniture and functional objects in the 1990s, some years after studying art at the École Nationale des Beaux-Arts in Bourges. He is a designer who works like an artist. His drawings, in which he explores lines, structures, contours, and colors, are on an equal footing with their three-dimensional realizations. Charpin designs simple, extremely precisely drafted objects which leave their function open to question—they are simultaneously abstract and concrete. The Frenchman, who lives in Ivry-sur-Seine near Paris, works for brands such as Ligne Roset, Sèvres, Zanotta, and Alessi, and his work is shown in design galleries such as Kreo in Paris.
www.pierrecharpin.com

David Chipperfield Architects
166
David Chipperfield (b. 1953) is a British architect who has realized many of his projects in Germany, including the Museum of Modern Literature in Marbach and the restoration of the Neues Museum in Berlin; he is currently engaged in remodeling the Folkwang Museum in Essen. Chipperfield studied at the Kingston School of Art and the Architectural Association School of Architecture (AA) in London and worked for Richard Rogers and Norman Foster before establishing his own firm in 1984, which now has branches in Berlin, Milan, and Shanghai. 2009 saw the completion of his new City of Justice complex in Barcelona, nine monolithic buildings with concrete load-bearing facades colored in different brown, yellow, and gray pastel tones.
www.davidchipperfield.co.uk

Nitzan Cohen
92, 205
Nitzan Cohen (b. 1973), who studied at the Avni Art Academy in Tel Aviv and the Design Academy Eindhoven, spent five years as project and studio manager for Konstantin Grcic in Munich before founding his own office in 2007. One of the first projects to be realized by the Israeli-born designer was the nan 15 modular shelf system composed of floor and backing elements. Cohen initially planned to produce the piece in graded colors, but it is currently only available in white, gray, and black.
www.nitzan-cohen.com

Committee
19, 234, 248
Clare Page (b. 1975) and Harry Richardson (b. 1975), who met as art students at the Liverpool School of Art, have been working together under the name of Committee since 2001. The functional and non-functional objects designed by the two Londoners are often assembled from materials they find at flea markets and on the street. Their "Kebab Lamps," which combine plastic animals, alarm clocks, porcelain vases, and other bric-à-brac, are carefully harmonized with respect to semantics and color. Working for the Spanish porcelain manufacturer Lladro, the artistic duo covered classical figurines with tiny pastel-colored blossoms. "The Lost Twin Ornaments" series was launched in 2009 and features unusual hybrid sculptures made of two mundane objects. The artists used a CAD program to compute the complex forms joining the objects.
www.gallop.co.uk

Tony Cragg
34, 72, 110, 137
British sculptor Tony Cragg (b. 1949) has been living in Wuppertal since 1977 and has been a professor at the Academy of Art in Düsseldorf since 1988. In 2009 he was appointed the school's dean. He has participated in Documenta twice and the Venice Biennale five times, and in 1988 he was awarded the Turner Prize. During the 1970s Cragg worked with found objects, plastic toys, and packaging, sometimes applying color and arranging them in patterns on the floor. Although he still experiments with unusual materials such as Kevlar, he generally favors traditional sculpting materials such as bronze and wood, which he cuts and arranges in layers to form extremely lively sculptures. These works call to mind vessels, columns, and spirals, and he generates some of their twisted, distorted, and rotating forms on the computer. Cragg often covers his sculptures with patterns or garish high-gloss colors, which homogenize the surface and conceal the material underneath.
www.tony-cragg.com

D

Thomas Demand
25, 179, 261
Berlin artist Thomas Demand (b. 1964) studied at the Munich and Düsseldorf art academies and at Goldsmiths College in London. Since the 1990s his strangely suggestive photographs have been exhibited all over the world. Demand uses images from the media as models for scenes he constructs in his studio out of cardboard, photographic paper, colored art paper, and tissue paper. He photographs these models and then destroys them. While the spaces and locations he refers to are reconstructed in great detail, their artificiality is unsettling—Demand omits the narrative elements present in the initial images, and the matt paper surfaces of his models do not reflect any light. These blank surfaces function as projection planes for the viewer's own images and memories.
www.thomasdemand.net

Saskia Diez
38, 91, 209
After completing an apprenticeship as a goldsmith, Munich-based designer Saskia Diez (b. 1976) studied industrial design at the Munich University of Applied Sciences. In 2006 the arm ring in her first collection met with unexpected success and she returned to jewelry. In her simple-looking yet highly refined designs, Diez often uses well-known forms from the jewelry-making tradition, but alters the material, surface, and composition. For instance, the individual elements in her diamond collection are made of bronze and glass, but are cast in diamond, emerald, and sapphire cuts, and plated in silver or gold. In contrast, the gaudily colored wooden balls in her "Wood" collection are given multiple coats of paint to create a mother-of-pearl surface. Diez has also worked with her husband, industrial designer Stefan Diez, on such projects as the "Papier" collection, which features handbags made of the synthetic paper Tyvek.
www.saskia-diez.de

Stefan Diez
60, 218, 263
Following an apprenticeship in cabinetmaking, Munich industrial designer Stefan Diez (b. 1971) studied at the Stuttgart State Academy of Art and Design. For two years he worked as assistant to Konstantin Grcic before opening his own studio in 2003. In addition to mounting exhibitions, he designs furniture, household articles, and bags for clients such as Rosenthal, elmarflötotto, Authentics, Schönbuch, e15, and Thonet.
www.stefan-diez.com

Tom Dixon
100, 169
Londoner Tom Dixon (b. 1959) is a design autodidact who attended the Chelsea School of Art for only a few months. He later taught himself to weld and went on to produce his first pieces of furniture from scrap metal. By the end of the eighties, he was already designing chairs for Cappellini and other well-known brands. From 2001 to 2008 he was creative director of Habitat. In 2002 he founded the Tom Dixon design studio with David Begg, which develops and produces mainly furniture and lighting. Dixon was one of the first furniture designers to utilize traditional materials and surface finishes used in industry and trades, such as copper, brass, enamel, anodized aluminum, and reflective, vapor-deposited metal coatings.
www.tomdixon.net

dRMM (de Rijke Marsh Morgan Architects)
53
Alex de Rijke (b. 1960), Philip Marsh (b. 1966), and Sadie Morgan (b. 1969) opened the dRMM office in London in 1995. In 2008 they took part in the Venice Architecture Biennale and they are currently participating in the design of the Olympic village to be built in London by 2012. A goal of dRMM architects is to build unconventional buildings using conventional materials—for instance, by developing innovative wooden constructions. They often use conspicuous color gradients to link large expanses or several structures, as seen in their housing complex in London's Wansey Street, where timber-backed facade panels made of fiber cement present a range of colors, from canary yellow to vermilion.
www.drmm.co.uk

E

William Eggleston
17, 43, 75, 142, 172
American artist William Eggleston (b. 1939) is regarded as the man who brought color to artistic photography. It had previously only been used in advertising and journalism. Eggleston began experimenting with color photography in the mid-1960s and the solo exhibition he held at MoMA in 1976 caused a sensation. Numerous photographers and filmmakers, including Wolfgang Tillmans and David Lynch, have drawn on his visual syntax, which is not based on a snapshot aesthetic—as critics have repeatedly claimed—but on a search for the perfect composition blending color and form. The often banal and mundane subject matter of his images is subordinated to color, which he manipulates and enhances in the editing process.
www.egglestontrust.com

Olafur Eliasson
37, 186, 219, 268
The Danish artist Olafur Eliasson (b. 1967) studied at the Royal Danish Academy of Art in Copenhagen, and in 1994 he moved to Berlin, where he is professor and director of the Institute for Experimental Studies at Berlin University of the Arts. Eliasson reconstructs the optical and physical phenomena of nature, often using simple tools such as mirrors, light, and water. Colors play a key role in his work. He is keenly interested in how they can be generated and perceived. In conjunction with his diverse projects, he has colored a river with a bilious green (though harmless) dye, created a yellow fog, and bathed entire museums in all colors of the spectrum using pulsating sheets of light.
www.olafureliasson.net

Andreas Exner
83, 102, 140, 196
Following a printer's apprenticeship, Frankfurt-born Andreas Exner (b. 1962) studied design and painting at the universities of applied sciences in Münster and Cologne before moving on to Frankfurt's Städelschule academy of fine art, where he attended the master class held by Jörg Immendorff. In his work, Exner explores the monochrome in a variety of ways, through both painting and installations. For his wall installations he uses monochromatic articles of clothing and sews material in a carefully selected second color into the openings in the garments. This technique refers to the work of Blinky Palermo, who also sewed together fabrics to form color fields. However, whereas Palermo stretched his cloth panels on orthogonal wooden frames, Exner hangs his everyday garments as they are on the wall.
www.andreasexner.net

F

ff-Architekten
40

Katharina Feldhusen (b. 1964) and Ralf Fleckenstein (b. 1964), who studied at the University of Technology in Darmstadt, have been working together as ff-Architekten in Berlin since 1996. Their work covers an extremely diverse range of projects, including a "Floating Home" design for Hamburg. One particularly notable example of their work is the Luckenwalde library, a converted railway station that they supplemented with an annexe. The structure is tilted along two axes and has a shimmering imbricated surface that reflects not only light and water but also passersby. Its golden color is generated by a special copper-aluminum alloy.
www.ff-architekten.de

Berta Fischer
21, 141

The sculptures by Berta Fischer (b. 1973) are minimalist, yet delicate and complex. The artist, who studied at the Karlsruhe University of Arts and Design and currently lives in Berlin, uses colors that are just as artificial looking as her transparent synthetic materials. She creates sculptures by cutting and bending heated panels of acrylic glass or by molding plastic industrial film. Light is refracted on the cut edges of the resulting spirals, balls, and abstract figures.
www.nourbakhsch.de, www.martinasbaek.com

Dan Flavin
125

From the time he first mounted a fluorescent tube diagonally on the wall of his New York studio on May 25, 1963, Dan Flavin (1933–1996) focused his artistic output on this one object. Today his light installations, which were often tied to a particular location, are regarded as some of the most important works of minimal art. The light source, or illuminant, is always a visible element of the installation, as are the space and its visitors, who are captured by the spreading colored light. Although Flavin only used fluorescent tubes with standard colors, he was able to produce ingenious perceptual illusions—for instance, by juxtaposing cold and warm light or integrating after-images.

Sylvie Fleury
45, 105, 122, 158

The Swiss artist Sylvie Fleury was born in Geneva in 1961, where she still lives today. From 1981 on she attended the Germain School of Photography in New York City but only started working as an artist in 1990. At the time she was the assistant to artist John Armleder. Fleury's staged presentations of glamour, fashion, and luxury immediately attracted attention. Her work plays with the fetishistic character and aesthetics of the world of commodities and features gilded shopping trolleys and car tires, oversized handbags, and stilettos. The surfaces she portrays are shiny, glittering, and garish, and her photographs are often shot through with the neon light of advertising signs.
www.sylviefleury.com

FORM Kouichi Kimura Architects
177, 201

Kouichi Kimura (b. 1960) founded the FORM architecture firm in Kusatu-City in Japan in 1994. He studied at Kyoto Art College and went on to specialize in residential buildings. His latest projects include the House of Vision (2008) and the House of Inclusion (2009) in the Shiga prefecture. Both structures are sheltered from the environment by a minimalistic, almost continuous, monochromatic facade—in homogeneous brown and gray respectively.
www.form-kimura.com

Katharina Fritsch
29, 74, 157, 187

Katharina Fritsch (b. 1956) studied at the Academy of Art in Düsseldorf and continues to live and work in Düsseldorf today. In 1995 she exhibited her work in the German pavilion at the Venice Biennale. Her objects and installations are among the best-known works of the contemporary art world. They include both life-size and larger-than-life iconic representations of animals and symbolic objects that are recognizable at first glance but nevertheless puzzling. Although the objects are highly realistic, their monochrome colors make them seem unreal.
www.matthewmarks.com

Front
94, 185, 204

The Swedish designers Sofia Lagerkvist (b. 1976), Charlotte von der Lancken (b. 1978), Anna Lindgren (b. 1977), and Katja Sävström (b. 1976) all studied at the Konstfack University College of Arts, Crafts and Design in Stockholm and have been working together since 2003 under the name of Front. Their conceptual designs attracted attention from the outset, in part because with each new project they question both their role as designers and design conventions. This extends to the integration in their design process of contextually foreign elements such as magic tricks and live animals, which help them to convey their ideas. Or they produce objects that move and play visual tricks, such as a cupboard equipped with a mechanism borrowed from billboard technology, which causes the pixel-like front side to change constantly. Front's clients include Moooi, Moroso, Established & Sons, Skitsch, and Porro.
www.frontdesign.se

Keisuke Fujiwara
130, 231

Although Keisuke Fujiwara (b. 1968) has been exhibiting at the Milan Furniture Fair for some years, he only recently began to attract the interest of Western furniture firms. The Japanese designer, who has had his own studio in Tokyo since 2001, experiments in particular with colors and surface structures, often using complicated production procedures to realize his ideas. His furniture series made of titanium is anodized in an electrolytic bath, which gives it a shimmering metallic surface with a color gradient that gently shifts from turquoise to blue and violet. Fujiwara took two months to wrap the famous Thonet No. 14 bentwood chair in six kilometers of thin thread. The resulting Spool Chair exhibits either soft blue or yellow tones.
www.keisukefujiwara.com

Massimiliano and Doriana Fuksas
56 – 57, 155

Massimiliano Fuksas (b. 1944) is an Italian architect of Lithuanian descent. Like his wife, Doriana, with whom he has been working since 1985, he studied at La Sapienza University in Rome. In 1967, two years prior to graduation, he established his first studio. Today he runs offices in Rome, Paris, Vienna, Frankfurt, and Shenzhen. When designing, Fuksas usually makes his initial freehand sketches using brightly colored pencils. However, when actually built, his designs rarely feature such colors. One exception is the concert hall in Strasbourg, which has an outer layer made of orange, translucent textile membrane. During the day the surface is opaque but by night interior lighting throws the supporting structure into stark relief.
www.fuksas.it

G

Rupprecht Geiger
28, 86, 120, 284 – 287

Rupprecht Geiger was born in Munich in 1908 and still lives there today. In spite of his interest in art he studied architecture in his hometown from 1926 to 1935. From 1965 to 1976 he held a professorship at the Academy of Art in Düsseldorf and took part in the Kassel Documenta four times. Geiger is particularly interested in the color red as an embodiment of light, energy, and the life-force. It is a recurring theme in his work.
www.storms-galerie.de

von Gerkan, Marg und Partner (gmp)
113

With a staff of 400, the Hamburg architectural office gmp Architekten headed by Volkwin Marg (b. 1936) and Meinhard von Gerkan (b. 1935) is the largest in Germany. Both men studied at the Braunschweig University of Technology and won their first big competition with a design for Berlin's Tegel Airport in 1965, the same year they opened their firm. The most important projects undertaken by gmp include the New Trade Fair in Leipzig and Berlin Central Station. In Cape Town, Durban, and Port Elizabeth they are building three stadiums for the 2010 Football World Cup. Another focus of their work is China, where in 2003 they won the competition to build Lingang New City, a satellite town for 800,000 residents near Shanghai. One of the first buildings to be completed is the High Tech Park, which features a facade they have structured simply yet effectively using ribbon glazing and horizontal bands in white and dark blue.
www.gmp-architekten.de

Liam Gillick
78, 222, 240, 247, 256

The installations and texts by Liam Gillick (b. 1964) are models of art practice that can be interpreted in very different ways. The British artist, who studied at the Hertfordshire School of Art and Design and at Goldsmiths College in London, explores the structures shaping our social, political, and economic reality, and designs scenarios of a postindustrial society. Examples of Gillick's conceptual models include minimalist shelf constructions and room dividers made of colored acrylic glass, MDF sheets, and aluminum railings, which Gillick sees as platforms for potential interaction and communication. Gillick exclusively uses colors from the limited palette provided by the industrial RAL system.
www.caseycaplangallery.com, www.estherschipper.com

Konstantin Grcic
195, 211, 288 – 291
Konstantin Grcic was born in Munich in 1965, where he has run his own design studio since 1991. He was educated in the UK, studied at the Royal College of Art in London, and worked for a year as an assistant to Jasper Morrison. His most well-known designs include the two chairs Chair_One (2004) and Myto (2008), and the lamp Mayday (1999). Grcic often limits his choice of colors to the RAL system commonly used in industry, thereby creating a color spectrum that defies prevailing color trends.
www.konstantin-grcic.com

Joachim Grommek
35, 46, 96, 167, 233
The paintings by Joachim Grommek (b. 1957), who studied at Braunschweig University of Art and currently lives and works in Berlin, are optical illusions. He paints not only striped images that look as if he has glued colored and transparent bands of tape on top of and next to each other, but also monochrome blocks in which the surface of the particle board support appears to have been left untreated along the edges of the painting. But both these effects are painted illusions, a deliberate attempt to bewilder viewers using layers of oil, acrylic, and high-gloss paint. Anyone who looks closely enough will find allusions to famous works of art history, by such artists as Malevich, Mondrian, Knoebel and Palermo.
www.vousetesici.nl

Katharina Grosse
48, 215, 230
Katharina Grosse (b. 1961) studied at the art academies in Münster and Düsseldorf with Norbert Tadeusz and Gotthard Graubner. She now lives in Berlin, where she is a professor at the Berlin-Weissensee School of Art. Grosse is known for her site-specific, temporary color installations, which she has been creating since the end of the 1990s. Rather than a brush, Grosse uses a spray-gun to apply paint, which considerably speeds up the work process due to the absence of surface friction—viewers can see the result in the flowing movements of her work. This technique produces atmospheric, expansive mists of color that dissolve edges and boundaries and produce almost hallucinatory color spaces. Grosse does not restrict herself to monochromes but also allows related and oppositional colors to clash in her work.
www.katharinagrosse.com

H

Zaha Hadid
70, 162
The architect Zaha Hadid (b. 1950), who comes from Iraq, is the first woman to have won the renowned Pritzker Architecture Prize. Hadid was a mathematics major at the American University in Beirut before studying architecture at the Architectural Association School of Architecture (AA) in London. There she worked in the Office for Metropolitan Architecture founded by Rem Koolhaas and in 1980 she opened her own studio. However, it was not until 1993 that the first of her spectacular buildings went up: the Vitra Fire Station in Weil am Rhein, Germany. While her early work was characterized by geometrical fissures, she later moved on to complex flowing forms, which are also a feature of her furniture design. Her work in this latter area includes limited editions for Established & Sons featuring high-gloss finishes.
www.zaha-hadid.com

Peter Haimerl
192
Munich architect Peter Haimerl (b. 1961), who opened his office in 1991 after studying at the Munich University of Applied Sciences, not only works on architecture and interior design projects but in recent years has also been responsible for large-scale research projects. These have given rise to the concept for the mobile and modular Cocobello studio and the futuristic urban concept Zoomtown, a city without cars in which people move around on one-man electric scooters. One design that has already been realized is the Black House in the Krailling municipality near Munich. Haimerl completely covered the 1930s single-family house with bitumen shingles—apart from the front side, which was plastered and painted snow-white.
www.urbnet.de

Jaime Hayón
85, 112, 152, 190, 214
Jaime Hayón (b. 1974) was still a teenager when he began earning money from design. In California, where the Spaniard was a professional skateboarder for some years, he designed graffiti-style graphics for skateboards and T-shirts. He later studied industrial design at the Istituto Europeo di Design (IED) in Madrid and the École Nationale Supérieure des Arts Décoratifs (ENSAD) in Paris and spent eight years working for Fabrica, the design think-tank set up by Benetton, before founding his own studio in 2004. Today Hayón is Spain's most renowned designer and has studios in London, Barcelona, and Treviso. He designs sculptural objects and theater sets featuring garish colors and glossy and glittering surfaces for clients such as Bisazza, Baccarat, Camper, Lladro, and Artquitect. He describes his style as "Mediterranean Digital Baroque."
www.hayonstudio.com

Herzog & de Meuron
103
The office headed by the Basel architects Jacques Herzog (b. 1950) and Pierre de Meuron (b. 1950) is regarded as one of the most influential in contemporary architecture. Both men graduated in 1975 from the Swiss Federal Institute of Technology (ETH) in Zurich, where they now hold professorships. They have been working together since 1978 and in 2001 were awarded the renowned Pritzker Prize. Herzog & de Meuron are known for, among other things, using facades as projection screens for patterns and material structures, as well as images and texts. In this context they sometimes employ unconventional materials such as copper, bronze or—as in the case of the multifunctional Forum Building in Barcelona—dyed concrete. The dark blue material was sprayed directly onto the structure, forming a flaked surface that creates an impression of coral.

Carsten Höller
27, 58, 95, 150, 235
German artist Carsten Höller (b. 1961) first studied agriculture and later, in 1993, took a postdoctoral degree in phytopathology, the study of plant illnesses. At times his art work recalls experimental lab situations, in which viewers voluntarily play the role of test subjects. With his expansive installations and optical illusions, Höller not only disconcerts viewers but animates them to interact with the work. His most famous objects include toadstools, birds, carnival attractions, and huge children's slides, all of which question how we construct our identities on the basis of sensory perception.
www.airdeparis.com, www.gagosian.com

J

Olav Christopher Jenssen
237, 265
The Norwegian painter Olav Christopher Jenssen (b. 1954) studied at the Oslo National Academy of the Arts and, after a sojourn in New York, moved to Berlin in 1982, where he still lives for the most part today. In 1992 he exhibited at Documenta 9 and since 2007 has held a professorship at the Braunschweig University of Art. Jenssen does not paint signs or figures; nor does he paint geometric constructions. His is a pure, abstract, tranquil form of painting, at times featuring more organic at others more crystalline forms. In part he uses templates to achieve a better contrast between individual color fields; his frequent use of white and pastel colors produces gentle color gradients.
www.galleririis.com

Hella Jongerius
98, 144, 163, 165, 203
Dutch designer Hella Jongerius (b. 1963) has played an important role in shifting the boundaries between design, crafts, and art. She interweaves historical and contemporary forms, motifs, and techniques to produce limited editions of serial objects, above all vases, crockery, furniture, and textiles. Shortly after completing her studies at the Design Academy Eindhoven in 1993, Jongerius attracted attention with her designs for Droog Design. In 2000 she opened her Jongeriuslab studio in Rotterdam. Of late she has been working from Berlin for clients such as Vitra, Ikea, Belux, Porzellan Manufaktur Nymphenburg, and Royal Tichelaar Makkum, and is represented by Galerie Kreo in Paris. She recently developed a new color concept for Vitra's furniture classics in which pastel tones dominate—as they do in many of her own designs.
www.jongeriuslab.com

Donald Judd
154
Donald Judd (1928–1994) is regarded as one of the most important artists of the minimal art movement. After studying philosophy and art history at New York's Columbia University, he first made a name for himself as an art critic. In the 1960s he exhibited his simple spatial volumes made from plywood for the first time. Focusing completely on aspects of material, color, and space, he designed open and closed cubes and cuboids, which he grouped on the floor or the wall. He often painted his wooden objects in cadmium red; in order to color aluminum and steel sheeting he had it galvanized, anodized, and enameled. His "Boxes," produced from the 1980s onwards, exhibit a range of intensive colors as do his furniture designs.
www.juddfoundation.org

K

Anish Kapoor
33, 52, 77, 156
Sculptor Anish Kapoor was born in Mumbai in 1954 and moved to London in 1972, where he studied at the Hornsey College of Art and the Chelsea College of Art and Design and which he still calls his home today. He was the recipient of the Turner Prize in 1991. Kapoor has always taken an interest in the relationship between material, space, color, and the viewer. He earned a name for himself with floor objects completely covered in intensely colored pigment powder. He later designed not only funnel- and membrane-like wall objects that suggest vast emptiness, but also spectacular monumental installations. One was shown at the Haus der Kunst in Munich and consisted of a twenty-ton red mass of wax and Vaseline that slid through the exhibition on rails. Kapoor favors the color red, which he regards as the color of matter and the human body.
www.anishkapoor.com

Ellsworth Kelly
24, 59, 227
American artist Ellsworth Kelly (b. 1923) is regarded as one of the most important color-field painters in art history. At a time when the first major U.S. art movement was evolving independently of Europe, he broke with the pack and began studying at the École des Beaux-Arts in Paris in 1948. Kelly did not return to the United States until 1954, and he now lives and works in Spencertown in upstate New York. He did his first monochrome paintings in 1952 and later created compositions out of several monochrome segments and blocks.
www.matthewmarks.com

Yves Klein
93, 115
In 1957 the French artist Yves Klein (1928–1962) made a single color, so-called International Klein Blue (IKB), into art. He developed this ultramarine blue with the help of chemists and subsequently had it patented. The pigments were dissolved in a new synthetic resin that enabled them to maintain the luminous intensity they have in powder form. In Klein's monochromatic works the color has an engulfing, almost immaterial effect. Klein, who never studied art, began painting monochromatic pictures in 1949, using colors that included pink and gold.
www.yveskleinarchives.org,
www.international-klein-blue.com

Imi Knoebel
55, 228, 273
Düsseldorf painter and installation artist Imi Knoebel (b. 1940) studied at the Werkkunstschule in Darmstadt and was a student of Joseph Beuys at the Academy of Art in Düsseldorf. He took part in Documenta 5, 6, 7, and 8. All his works are concerned with the question of the non-representational image, how it is constituted, and what reactions it can evoke from viewers. Knoebel repeatedly makes reference to forerunners of his approach such as Malevich, Mondrian, and Newman, whose work he also comments on ironically. His installations are often made up of juxtaposed or polygonal boards, which he stacks or leans against walls. He first began working with color in the 1970s. Since then he has created several groups of works using only primary colors or bright orange anti-corrosive primer.

L

Lederer + Ragnarsdóttir + Oei
108
The Stuttgart office run by Arno Lederer (b. 1947), Jórunn Ragnarsdóttir (b. 1957) and Marc Oei (b. 1962) is making a stand against the emphasis on transparency and the glass envelopes predominant in contemporary architecture. The three architects, who all studied in Stuttgart, confront these tendencies with closed, physically emphatic structures featuring masonry facades and accentuated surfaces: brickwork, corrugated aluminum, slate and, tiles. They completely covered the Gustav-von-Schmoller vocational school with luminous dark-blue tiles, a strategy they also employed when extending the municipal court building in Pforzheim.
www.lederer-ragnarsdottir-oei.de

Amanda Levete
16
British architect and designer Amanda Levete (b. 1955) ran the London firm Future Systems for twenty years together with her husband, Jan Kaplicky (1937–2009). The office was a pioneer in so-called "blob" architecture. In 2009 Levete established her own studio, Amanda Levete Architects, and has designed limited edition objects for Established & Sons and other design companies. In 2008, for example, she created a collection of furniture for the corners of rooms, using forms that are just as fluid and organic as those of her architecture. Her fiberglass corner shelf, North, features a garish greenish-yellow fluorescent surface.
www.amandalevetearchitects.com

Arik Levy
118, 147, 180
Arik Levy (b. 1963) is not only an industrial designer but also a stage designer, a filmmaker, and an artist. His Paris-based firm, L Design, also develops, among other things, corporate identities and exhibition designs. Born in Israel, Levy arrived in Switzerland in 1988 to study industrial design at the European branch of the Art Center College of Design in Vevey. In 1997 he founded L Design with Pippo Lionni. The firm's clients include Baccarat, Swarovski, e15, Ligne Roset, Vitra, and Desalto. His signature Rock pieces, which he has been creating since 2005, are crystalline furniture sculptures incorporating several planes that refract light differently and thus create a moving surface. L Design has the Rocks produced in mirror-polished stainless steel, wenge wood and with textile coverings in limited editions.
www.ldesign.fr

M

Maison Martin Margiela
66, 76, 89, 189, 198, 212, 252
Paris's Maison Martin Margiela (MMM) is regarded as one of the most influential fashion labels of the last two decades. It was founded in 1988 by the Belgian Martin Margiela (b. 1957), who had previously studied fashion design at the Royal Academy of Fine Arts and worked as an assistant to Jean-Paul Gaultier. Since 2002 MMM has been part of the Diesel Group. From the beginning MMM attracted attention not only because it commented on fashion-industry rules but also because it broke them. Margiela turned on its head the understanding of history prevailing in the industry by giving existing garments a second life, cutting them up and remodeling them or using them to reproduce historical designs. His strategy for maintaining anonymity includes requiring MMM staff to wear white lab coats and covering parts of his collections in matt white.
www.martinmargiela.com

Mansilla+Tuñón
264
The architect duo of Luis M. Mansilla (b. 1959) and Emilio Tuñón Álvarez (b. 1958) studied at the Escuela Técnica Superior de Arquitectura de Madrid (ETSAM) and opened their joint office in the same city in 1992. They have taught at a number of institutions, including Harvard, Princeton, and Frankfurt's Städelschule academy of fine art. In 2007 their design for the MUSAC Contemporary Art Museum of Castilla and León in the city of León won them the renowned Mies van der Rohe Award. The buildings are clad on one side with facades made of colored glass elements in warm, finely graded tones. In order to choose the colors Mansilla+Tuñón used a computer to examine the 3,351 different color tones found in the glass mosaics in the León Cathedral. They then selected a number of these and transferred them onto glass.
www.mansilla-tunon.com

Eva Marguerre
80
Eva Marguerre (b. 1983) is a German product designer who has been studying at the Karlsruhe University of Arts and Design since 2004. She has worked for Luigi Colani and Stefan Diez and exhibited at the Kortrijk Design Biennale and the DMY Design Festival in Berlin. While studying under Stefan Diez, Marguerre produced "Nido," which comprises a series of interconnected filigree stools made of wrapped fiberglass strands permeated with bright red polyester resin. The fiberglass manufacturer Masson is now producing four variations of this extremely light and surprisingly stable form of seating.
www.eva-marguerre.de

Mass Studies, Minsuk Cho
160–161
The South Korean architect Minsuk Cho (b. 1966) founded the Mass Studies architecture firm in Seoul in 2003 after studying at Seoul's Yonsei University and New York's Columbia University. He also worked for a time for the Office for Metropolitan Architecture run by Rem Koolhaas, before opening his first practice in New York with James Slade in 1998. Since returning to South Korea, Cho has worked on several large-scale projects in Seoul, including the city's new City Hall. At present he is working on the South Korean Pavilion for the World Expo 2010 in Shanghai. One of his most notable designs is for a building in Seoul that includes a shop for the Belgian fashion designer Ann Demeulemeester; one side of the facade is completely covered by perennial Japanese boxwood.
www.massstudies.com

JÜRGEN MAYER H.
15
Jürgen Mayer H. (b. 1965) studied architecture at Stuttgart University, Cooper Union in New York City, and Princeton University. He has run his own architectural office in Berlin since 1996, designing not only buildings, but also art installations, interiors, and furniture. His best-known design is the Metropol Parasol, a mushroom-shaped complex spanning a central square in Seville. Scheduled for completion in 2010, it will be a market hall, a canopy, and a vast sculpture all in one. Jürgen Mayer H. works with patterns of encrypted data and columns of numbers and has taken a special interest in color. His designs incorporate the reflective colors of road markings, as well as phosphorescent and thermochromatic paints. For the facade of the Karlsruhe University student cafeteria, he used a synthetic-looking yellowish green, which disguises the underlying material—polyurethane-coated wood.
www.jmayerh.de

Willy Müller Architects (WMA)
269
The Argentinian-born architect Willy Müller (b. 1961) moved to Spain in 1985 to study at the Escola Tècnica Superior d'Arquitectura de Barcelona (ETSAB). He founded his own practice in 1996 and was quickly able to acquire international projects in countries including Russia, Brazil, and Mexico. However, one of his most striking designs was for his adopted hometown of Barcelona: the new building for the Mercabarna-Flor wholesale flower market, which features a multi-folded zinc roof framed by a multi-colored band. The band is made of vertical strips in a wide range of colors and is visible from a long way off. It continues in the interior of the building as a structuring element.
www.willy-muller.com

Kostas Murkudis
232
Berlin fashion designer Kostas Murkudis was born in Dresden in 1959 to Greek parents. He moved to West Berlin as an adolescent, where he studied chemistry and later fashion design at the Lette Foundation. He worked briefly for Wolfgang Joop and then as an assistant to Helmut Lang before founding his own label. Every year Murkudis produces two new collections for women and men. However, his 96dresses made from silk are conceived as a permanent collection. In the cooler seasons, several color variations of these light summer frocks can be worn over one another, with the choice covering a spectrum of 96 tones. In 2006 Murkudis applied the same concept to a short-sleeved man's shirt.
www.kostasmurkudis.net

MVRDV
47, 126–127
Winy Maas (b. 1959), Jacob van Rijs (b. 1964), and Nathalie de Vries (b. 1965) founded MVRDV in Rotterdam one year after graduating from the Delft University of Technology. The architecture office, which was responsible for the Dutch pavilion at Expo 2000 in Hanover, is now involved in projects all over the world. MVRDV is renowned for the conceptual and experimental nature of its architecture and also for its use of color. Some of its buildings give the impression of being bathed in color. One notable example is the bright orange Studio Thonik in Amsterdam, which attracted energetic protests from those living nearby. The dispute over the color even came to court, with the result that the municipality eventually paid half of the cost of having the building repainted green. The firm struck an equally strident tone when remodeling the roof area of the Didden Village residential complex in Rotterdam, adding a number of rooftop "cottages" surrounded by a low wall and covered with a layer of sky-blue polyurethane.
www.mvrdv.nl

N

Hiroshi Nakamura & NAP Architects
210
Japanese architect Hiroshi Nakamura (b. 1974) founded the firm NAP Architects in Tokyo in 2003 after studying at Japan's Meiji University and working for Kengo Kuma. Nakamura now works on building projects both at home and abroad in places such as Kuwait and Beijing. He also develops interior designs, such as that for the Nike Tokyo Design Studio. His light designs are particular notable. The House SH he designed is located in a residential neighborhood of Tokyo that is so densely built up that natural lighting could only be obtained from above. Nakamura pushed out one side of the building to create a convex hollow, which now allows in varying types of light depending on the weather. Another example is the bathroom in the Necklace House in Yamagata, the external walls of which are equipped with innumerable small openings, allowing small points of light to flood the entire space.
www.nakam.info

Sirous Namazi
184, 239
Swedish artist Sirous Namazi was born in Iran in 1970. He studied at the Malmö Art Academy and now lives in Stockholm. In 2007 he represented Sweden in the Nordic Pavilion at the Venice Biennale. Namazi works with a highly diverse range of media. His modular sculptures made from colorfully enameled lattice structures, for instance, can be seen as a reinterpretation of the Minimal Art of Sol LeWitt. Another group of works consists of photographs that Namazi took at night in an unlit Stockholm apartment. At first glance they appear completely black, but the longer you look the more you can make out the silhouettes of the individual pieces of furniture and other objects in the space.
www.sirousnamazi.com

Nendo
208, 250
Nendo is the design studio founded by Oki Sato (b. 1977), who grew up in Toronto and studied architecture at Waseda University in Tokyo. In 2002 he opened his first office there, which has now become one of the most internationally renowned and successful in Japan. Nendo works in the fields of product, furniture, and packaging design, architecture and interior architecture and in 2005 established a branch office in Milan. Its clients include Swedese, Moroso, Cappellini, Boffi, Quodes, Puma, and Toyota. In 2008 the studio designed the Cabbage Chair made of pleated paper for the 21_21 Design Sight design museum in Tokyo. The resin-coated, folded material is a waste product generated by the manufacture of pleated fabric. Nendo rolled the paper into a cylinder and cut it vertically halfway down one side so that the layers could be folded back one after the other, thus converting a roll of waste material into an elastic, yet stable form of seating without using any other resources.
www.nendo.jp

Jean Nouvel
114, 238
Jean Nouvel (b. 1945) studied at the Écoles des Beaux-Arts in Bordeaux and Paris and had already opened his first office with François Seigneur in 1970, two years prior to graduating. Today he is one of France's most internationally renowned architects. His current firm, Ateliers Jean Nouvel, has a staff of more than 100. Nouvel often stages his buildings using colorful facades and colored light, good examples of which can be seen in the Copenhagen Concert Hall with its meshed blue fiberglass facade, and the iridescent Torre Agbar in Barcelona. This 140-meter high-rise is clad in aluminum plates finished in 40 different color shades. Additional light reflections are created by glass panels positioned at different angles. At night the tower is illuminated by LEDs.
www.jeannouvel.fr

O

OFIS Arhitekti
262
Rok Oman (b. 1970) and Špela Videčnik (b. 1971) founded the Slovenian architecture firm OFIS in 1998 after they had both studied in Ljubljana and at the Architectural Association School of Architecture (AA) in London. Since then they have specialized particularly in residential buildings and have been able to realize a number of highly unusual projects in Slovenia. These include a public-housing complex in Izola on the Adriatic coast. The building features a honeycomb pattern of loggias shaded by semi-transparent awnings in different colors. These create different atmospheres inside the apartments and lend the facade its varied appearance.
www.ofis-a.si

Valerio Olgiati
174–175, 206
Architect Valerio Olgiati (b. 1958) quickly gained recognition with numerous unusual building projects in the Swiss canton of Graubünden, where he was born. He studied at the Swiss Federal Institute of Technology (ETH) in Zurich and worked for a time in Los Angeles before opening his own office in Zurich, which he moved to Flims in Graubünden in 2008. Since 2002 he has held a professorship at the Università della Svizzera italiana in Mendrisio, and since 2009 he has held the Kenzo Tange Chair at Harvard University. One of his projects realized in Graubünden is the studio built for the musician Linard Bardill, the red-brown facade of which is adorned with numerous cast rose ornamentations.
www.olgiati.net

P

Verner Panton
87, 245
The furniture and environments by Verner Panton (1926–1998) had a decisive influence on the utopian-psychedelic design of the sixties and seventies. The

Danish designer, who studied architecture at the Royal Danish Academy of Fine Arts in Copenhagen while also working as an assistant to Arne Jacobsen, founded his own studio in 1955, which he moved to Basel in 1963. His most well-known design, the Panton Chair, was already produced in 1959/60: a sculptural cantilever chair that was the first of its kind to be made from a single piece of plastic. Panton also designed cavern-like living environments, such as Visiona 2, which are distinguished by the excessive application of colors.
www.verner-panton.com

Charlotte Posenenske
32, 62, 119, 257
Charlotte Posenenske (1930–1985) was one of the most important German artists of the 1960s, but it is only recently that she has been rediscovered, thanks to Documenta 12 and other exhibitions. In 1950 she began studying under Willi Baumeister at the Stuttgart State Academy of Art and Design, after which she worked as a stage designer. Although her works are closely linked to minimal art, they also have a radical democratic dimension: during her lifetime Posenenske not only had them mass-produced, but also sold them at cost. In keeping with this philosophy, she used only inexpensive industrial materials and a reduced color palette: first the standard colors of felt-tip pens and adhesive tapes; then (for her wall objects) the red, yellow, blue, and black of the RAL color chart; and, finally, the material colors of cardboard, pressboard, and sheet steel. Posenenske gave up art in 1968 in order to study sociology, saying that "Art cannot contribute to solving pressing social problems."
www.mehdi-chouakri.com

R

Michael Reiter
226, 271
Colored textile tape is the preferred material used by Frankfurt-based artist Michael Reiter (b. 1952) for his site-specific installations and wall objects. Reiter, who studied at the Academy of Fine Arts in Nuremberg, sews together pieces of standard textile tape to form geometric figures, or stretches them into bands several meters long extending through exhibition spaces, where the shiny, sometimes fluorescent, colors are reflected onto the white walls. Traces of the artist's work process are visible in the form of hanging threads, which offset the strict linearity of his structures.
www.reiter-michael.de

Anselm Reyle
88, 151, 199, 270, 304–307
Unlike most of his artistic contemporaries, the Berlin artist Anselm Reyle (b. 1970) does not even attempt to avoid sensationalism, decoration, and kitsch. On the contrary, these are concepts that this painter and sculptor, who trained at the Karlsruhe University of Arts and Design, deliberately exploits, producing works that include cheap glossy foil, glittering car paints, and fluorescent colors. His stripe and material compositions draw on the work of modernist artists such as Otto Freundlich and Ellsworth Kelly.
www.gagosian.com, www.alminerechgallery.com, www.themoderninstitute.com, www.andersen-s.de

Gerhard Richter
200, 229, 249, 296–299
Gerhard Richter (b. 1932) has been plumbing the possibilities of painting since the early 1960s. He first came to critical attention with his portrayals of black-and-white newspaper photographs. A short time later he began producing series of color fields, initially based on conventional color-sample cards of house painters; he went on to produce gestural abstractions and monochromatic, gray canvases, which he sees as expressions of indifference and the refusal to make a statement. In 1961 Richter fled the GDR for West Germany and studied under Karl Otto Götz at the Academy of Art in Düsseldorf until 1964. Now living in Cologne, the painter has taken part in the Documenta six times. In 1997 he was awarded the Golden Lion by the Venice Biennale.
www.gerhard-richter.com

Rojkind Arquitectos
36, 68–69, 73
Although the projects by Mexican architect Michel Rojkind (b. 1969) have as yet been realized mainly in his own country, his work has gained an enthusiastic international following. Rojkind has an office in Mexico City, where he creates his unusual, in part experimental designs. For a project in Tecamachalco he placed a second house on the roof of a house from the 1960s. The new structure was clad in curved steel plates and painted with bright red car paint. Rojkind has also designed a chocolate museum for Nestlé featuring a 300-meter-long facade in the same bright red. The museum houses a research center with curved niches that provide views of the intensive yellow and orange interior.
www.rojkindarquitectos.com

S

Sauerbruch Hutton
254–255, 260, 280–283
The work of the architecture firm Sauerbruch Hutton has become renowned for the particular color concepts developed by its founders, the most prominent examples of which are the GSW headquarters building in Berlin (1999) and the Brandhorst Museum in Munich (2009). The German Matthias Sauerbruch (b. 1955) and the Briton Louisa Hutton (b. 1957) founded their firm in London in 1989, where both of them had previously studied at the Architectural Association School of Architecture (AA); in 1993 they moved to Berlin.
www.sauerbruchhutton.com

Scholten & Baijings
109, 236
Stefan Scholten (b. 1972), who studied at the Dutch Design Academy Eindhoven, and the autodidact Carole Baijings (b. 1973) founded their design studio in Amsterdam in the year 2000. In their product and furniture designs they often make use of traditional handcraft techniques, which they incorporate in their modern design language. One example is the series Colour Plaids, large woolen blankets in luminous colors that are woven by the Dutch weaving firm De Ploeg. The gentle color gradients form progressions that are repeatedly interrupted by robust stripes of color.
www.scholtenbaijings.com

Schulz & Schulz Architekten
153
The brothers Ansgar (b. 1966) and Benedikt (b. 1968) Schulz have been working together in their architectural practice in Leipzig since 1992. Both of them studied at the RWTH Aachen University, after which Ansgar went on to study at the Escuela Técnica Superior de Arquitectura (ETSA) in Madrid and Benedikt at the UC de Asunción in Paraguay. One focus of their work is the design of public buildings. In the town of Chemnitz, for instance, they remodeled a police station, cladding the building with shimmering silver panels. They also opened a section of the facade to create a new main entrance, which, like the waiting area, they designed completely in the green associated with the German police force. Access to the building is now via an outside staircase also colored in a rich green.
www.schulz-und-schulz.com

Tilo Schulz
171, 181
Tilo Schulz was born in Leipzig in 1972. As an artist he deals with the clichés and political implications of abstract and formalistic modernism. He is an autodidact who began producing non-figurative paintings in the early nineties. Since 2005 he has been working on "Intarsien" (Inlays), a series of small-format pictures he creates using grained veneers and thin strips of light-colored wood. These austere compositions can be read both as an ironically affirmative response to abstract painting and as an engagement with the surfaces of the representative.
www.tiloschulz.com

Maarten Van Severen
23, 133
Belgian designer Maarten Van Severen (1956–2005) left behind a small yet striking body of work. The material, form, and colors of his purist furniture are harmoniously combined, and some pieces were only manufactured after his death. The son of constructivist painter Dan Van Severen, Maarten studied architecture but did not complete his degree. He began designing furniture in 1986 and shortly after also started producing small batches of his furniture in his Ghent workshop. He was placed under contract at Vitra in 1996, which resulted in the first mass production of his designs. Additional clients included edra, Pastoe, and Kartell.

Jerszy Seymour
129
The Canadian Jerszy Seymour (b. 1968) grew up in London and studied industrial design at the Royal College of Art. He then moved to Milan and later Berlin, where he has lived since 2004. Although he produces work for manufacturers such as Magis and Moulinex, he devotes much of his time to his own conceptual projects, which are characterized by an approach that is both utopian and absurdist. Among other things, he has attempted to create a new artificial material from potatoes, with which everyone can make their own furniture and other everyday articles. Until then, his preferred material was polyurethane foam, which he poured over pieces of furniture or shaped into amorphous forms and entire spatial installations.
www.jerszyseymour.com

SPLITTERWERK
22, 135
SPLITTERWERK is a group of Graz architects and artists founded in 1988. Its members create installations, media projections, paintings, and architectural projects. As can be seen from the few architectural designs built to date, SPLITTERWERK concentrates primarily on computer-generated patterns, as well as on experimental surfaces and coatings. Some of its buildings are covered so uniformly with colored patterns and structures that they appear two-dimensional. Other projects are dominated by a single color, such as Roter Laubfrosch (Red Tree Frog) and Grüner Laubfrosch (Green Tree Frog). In the Wohnstück Übelbach complex, all the elements attached to the houses, such as balconies and stairwells, are painted in the building's signal yellow, which is otherwise only visible shimmering through the protective wooden slats of the facades.
www.splitterwerk.at

Studio Job
41, 170, 188, 216, 246
The Antwerp-based Studio Job consists of Job Smeets (b. 1970 in Belgium) and Nynke Tynagel (b. 1977 in the Netherlands). The partners studied at the Design Academy Eindhoven, with Tynagel concentrating on graphic design and Smeets on product design. Since Studio Job was founded in 1998, it has explored the border zone between art and design. In cooperation with design galleries such as Moss in New York and manufacturers such as Royal Tichelaar Makkum, Smeets and Tynagel have designed kitschy, ironic objects that are produced laboriously by hand as limited editions or unique works. This work includes furniture and oversized objects with traditional religious, folkloric, and fairytale motifs combining representations of different subjects such as rockets and nuclear power plants. The materials they use for these pieces, including gilded and rusted surfaces and tin, were long frowned upon in design circles.
www.studiojob.be

Studio Schellmann Furniture
26, 202
The Munich gallery Edition Schellmann, which is run by Jörg Schellmann (b. 1944) and has additional offices in Berlin and New York City, has been publishing contemporary fine art editions since 1969. In 2008 it established Schellmann Furniture to produce limited editions of furniture designed by artists such as Joseph Beuys, Gerhard Merz, Donald Judd, and Liam Gillick. Jörg Schellmann has also designed some of the furniture using standardized industrial materials such as steel piping, MDF board, and plastic Euro-Fix crates. The minimalist design of these pieces refers back to 1990s minimalism and the "ready-made" strategies of Achille and Pier Giacomo Castiglioni.
www.schellmannfurniture.com

Shaan Syed
51, 107, 149
Painter Shaan Syed was born in Toronto in 1975 and now lives in London. He studied at Concordia University in Montreal, Ontario College of Art and Design in Toronto, and, until 2006, at Goldsmiths College in London. Syed's painting has changed radically within a short period of time: from figurative to non-representative works, which in part reference the painting characteristic of the 1960s. One of his latest series, entitled "Shoegazer," comprises pure color painting and incorporates luminous color gradients.
www.shaansyed.com

T

Tham & Videgård Hansson Arkitekter
44, 90, 144
Bolle Tham (b. 1970) and Martin Videgård Hansson (b. 1968) opened their architecture office in Stockholm in 1999. Their projects cover a range of fields, including urban planning, interior architecture, as well as exhibition and furniture design. When renovating a ten-room apartment in Stockholm, they used particularly lush colors. The individual rods in the ash-wood herringbone parquet were painted in different shades of orange, red, yellow, green, and violet, and laid to create color gradients between the rooms. A result of the seamless blending of the parquet with the wall paneling is that not only the individual rooms but also the walls and flooring appear to flow into one another.
www.tvh.se

Wolfgang Tillmans
79, 82, 121, 128, 143, 266
German photographer Wolfgang Tillmans (b. 1968), who studied from 1990 to 1992 at the Bournemouth and Poole College of Art and Design, has become internationally renowned for his pictures of rave and gay scenes. Since the early nineties he has worked for magazines such as *ID*, *Interview*, and *The Face*. In 2000 he was awarded the Turner Prize. He holds a professorship at Frankfurt's Städelschule academy of fine art and lives in London and Berlin. Tillmans is constantly searching for beauty—in his apparently random, but in fact carefully staged, figurative photography, but also in abstract photographs produced in a darkroom without a camera. Tillmans experiments with light, colors, and different types of photographic paper, creating monochromatic and luminous colored images in which color fans out in striations, thin threads, and progressions. Some of his latest series feature photographic paper folded once or several times.
www.tillmans.co.uk

James Turrell
65
The light artist James Turrell (b. 1943) comes from a Quaker family and studied psychology, mathematics, art history, and later art in the Californian town of Claremont. In 1966 he began developing his first light projections and light spaces. In 1974 he purchased an extinct volcano crater in the Arizona desert, where he still lives today. There he digs underground spaces and shafts opening to the sky that heighten the experience of constantly fluctuating celestial light. Making the reality of light visible is also the focus of Turrell's light installations. In these works, homogeneously colored light generated using concealed light sources paradoxically takes on a material, almost corporeal character, forming an indeterminate space whose limits are indiscernible.

U

UNStudio
54, 71, 292–295
When Ben van Berkel (b. 1957) and Caroline Bos (b. 1959) gave the name UNStudio to the firm they founded in Amsterdam in 1998, they were also defining their enterprise's leitmotif and way of working. The letters UN stand for United Net for Architecture, Urbanism, and Infrastructure, and the name is intended to emphasize UNStudio's claim to constitute a comprehensive network working with a range of specialists including designers, urban planners, theorists, and managers on progressive architectural projects. Their work is particularly characterized by computer-generated design techniques, whether they are designing buildings such as the Mercedes-Benz-Museum in Stuttgart, or the MYchair. The designers use crystalline and curved forms to define landscapes, cities, and spaces. The dominance of these monoliths is further underscored by intense, monochromatic colors.
www.unstudio.com

W

Richard Woods
49, 61, 148, 207, 258
The British artist Richard Woods (b. 1966) is a graduate of the Slade School of Fine Art in London and draws on the clichés of British furnishing and architectural styles. He creates rough imitations of building materials and textures such as herringbone parquet, red bricks, floral wallpapers, and half-timbering. He applies these to floors, walls, and entire building facades, creating a parody of the British country style that seems to have been borrowed from the world of Playmobil or comics. Woods' most recent work for the London design firm of Established & Sons comprised a series of laminate surfaces for furniture with gaudy colors and a wood grain pattern.
www.richardwoodsstudio.com

Y

yes architecture
30–31
The two architects Ruth Berktold (b. 1967) and Marion Wicher (b. 1966) first met as students in the Masters program in advanced architectural design at Columbia University in New York City. In 2002 they founded the joint office yes architecture, which has branches in Munich, Graz, and New York City. Berktold and Wicher often take an interdisciplinary approach to their work and, in addition to architecture, they design interiors, exhibition stands, and objects. Their most striking design to date is the mail distribution center of the Austrian post office in Trofaiach, which features a metal facade in the postal service's signature yellow.
www.yes-architecture.com

Tokujin Yoshioka
213
Following his studies at the Kuwasawa Design School (KDS) in Tokyo, Tokujin Yoshioka (b. 1967) worked in the studios of the furniture designer Shiro Kuramata and the fashion designer Issey Miyake before establishing his own studio in 2000. Since then his work has been attracting great interest, for instance at the Milan Furniture Fair, and his clients include Moroso, Driade, and Swarovski. Yoshioka's main interest is not in the final product but rather in creating design and production processes comparable with those found in nature. He allows crystal structures to grow into furniture, or bakes a chair made of polyester fibers in an oven like a loaf of bread. The colors he uses come from the

material itself, such as the white of paper and the transparent, highly reflective surfaces of fiberglass. www.tokujin.com

Z

Peter Zimmermann
111, 251, 253
The painter Peter Zimmermann (b. 1956) was born in Cologne and studied at the State Academy of Art and Design in Stuttgart. From 2002 to 2007 he held a professorship at the Academy of Media Arts in Cologne. Zimmermann made a name for himself in the 1980s with a series of Book Cover Paintings, which he produced by painting on the covers of books such as travel guides and atlases. For some time now he has been translating found images from magazines and the internet into paintings that recall the Abstract Expressionism of the fifties. He reworks the material with Photoshop to the point where the images dissolve into diffuse striations, color fields, and abstract structures and he then transfers them onto canvas using layers of pigmented epoxy resin. The glossy surface that results intensifies the effect of the luminous colors.
www.peterzimmermann.com

Beat Zoderer
223, 242, 259
The Swiss artist Beat Zoderer (b. 1955) flouts the strict rules and laws of concrete and constructive art playfully and with a good dose of humor. He lives in Wettingen in the canton of Aargau, where he constructs his images using office materials and waste material such as adhesive tape, corrugated cardboard, adhesive labels, and polystyrene balls, forming them into overlapping layers, arranging them into patterns, or even copying pictures by Max Bill and Picasso. Zoderer only needs three colored paper protectors, which he slides into one another, to create an intensely luminous color-field image.

Thank you!

We would like to express our particular gratitude to the designers, artists, and architects featured in this publication. Our thanks also go to the photographers who have generously given us access to their work, and to all the museums, art associations, and galleries that have helped us in researching and obtaining pictures.

We would also like to thank all those who have contributed to the publication of this book with their ideas, criticism, and patience: Helge Aszmoneit, Frankfurt am Main; Pascal Kress, Frankfurt am Main; Berit Liedtke, Basel; Ulrike Ruh, Basel; Katrin Tüffers, Frankfurt am Main; Markus Weisbeck, Frankfurt am Main; Peter Wesner, Frankfurt am Main.

Interviews need time, and we would therefore like to express our warm thanks to our interviewees, who so patiently answered questions on the subject of color: Ronan & Erwan Bouroullec, Paris; Fernando Campana, Studio Campana, São Paulo; Konstantin Grcic, Munich; Louisa Hutton, Sauerbruch Hutton, Berlin; Anselm Reyle, Berlin.

For their preparation of the pictorial material and information required for such a publication and for their enthusiastic input we would like to thank: Agentur V, Berlin; Air de Paris, Paris; Andersen's Contemporary, Berlin; Dr. Burkhard Brunn, Frankfurt am Main; Galerie Daniel Buchholz, Cologne; Cheim & Read, New York; Anthony Cragg Office, Wuppertal; Dogenhaus Galerie, Leipzig; e15, Oberursel; Studio Olafur Eliasson, Berlin; Established & Sons, London; Rupprecht Geiger Archiv, Munich; Liam Gillick, London; Hayon Studio, Barcelona; Friedhelm Hütte, Frankfurt am Main; Galerie Michael Janssen, Berlin; Luzia Kälin, Frankfurt am Main; Casey Kaplan, New York; Studio Anish Kapoor, London; Ellsworth Kelly Studio Archives, New York; Yves Klein Archives, Paris; Galerie Kreo, Paris; Sophie Lovell, Berlin; Matthew Marks Gallery, New York; Galerie Nordenhake Berlin/Stockholm, Berlin; Galerie Giti Nourbakhsch, Berlin; Frank Polley, Hamburg; Almine Rech Gallery, Brussels/Paris; Atelier Anselm Reyle, Berlin; Atelier Gerhard Richter, Cologne; Galleri Riis, Oslo; Galerie Thaddaeus Ropac Salzburg – Paris, Salzburg; Esther Schipper, Berlin; Galerie Horst Schuler, Düsseldorf; Sprüth Magers Berlin London, Berlin; Walter Storms Galerie, Munich; Studio Job, Antwerp; Vitra, Weil am Rhein; VOUS ETES ICI, Amsterdam

Cover illustration:
Liam Gillick, *Between Kalmar and Udevalla*, 2008
Courtesy of Liam Gillick and Casey Kaplan, New York

About the editors

The interior architect *Barbara Glasner* is a consultant and freelance curator for design and architecture based in Frankfurt am Main, Germany. From 2001 to 2007, in collaboration with the German Design Council, she supervised the various editions of the highly successful design project "ideal house cologne," where internationally renowned designers such as Zaha Hadid, Hella Jongerius, Konstantin Grcic, Ronan & Erwan Bouroullec, Naoto Fukasawa and Dieter Rams presented their visions for future living, at the International Furniture Fair Cologne. Her expertise in this field is further demonstrated by the various exhibitions she has curated and her participation in exhibitions, trade fairs, and events worldwide. In 2008, together with Ursula Schöndeling und Petra Schmidt, Glasner edited the book *Patterns 2. Design, Art and Architecture* published by Birkhäuser Verlag.

Petra Schmidt is an independent author and consultant in Frankfurt am Main. She teaches theory of design at the Karlsruhe University of Arts and Design and writes for art and design magazines such as *art* and *Frame*. After studying theater, film, and media in Frankfurt, she worked for various design firms and was editor in chief of the design journal *form* from 1999 to 2007. She is co-editor of the books *Patterns* and *Patterns 2. Design, Art and Architecture,* published by Birkhäuser Verlag in 2005 and 2008 respectively. Her most recent publication is the book *Unfolded. Paper in Design, Art, Architecture and Industry*, which she wrote in collaboration with Nicola Stattmann (Birkhäuser 2009).

About the authors

Jens Asthoff is a freelance author and critic who lives in Hamburg. He writes for numerous art magazines including *Artforum*, *Camera Austria*, *Kunstforum*, *Kultur & Gespenster* and contributes articles on contemporary art to catalogues and art publications.

Markus Frenzl is a design critic as well as a design consultant with a focus on consultation, conception, strategy, and corporate publishing. He contributes to both specialist and general magazines such as *Design Report* and *Elle Decoration* on the subjects of everyday and design culture and has held a number of lecturing positions in design theory.

Dr. Oliver Herwig works as a freelance journalist in Munich and writes for the *Süddeutsche Zeitung*, the *Frankfurter Rundschau*, *Monopol*, *GQ* and other publications. He also teaches design theory at the universities of Karlsruhe and Linz, and communications in Basel.

Silke Hohmann is an art critic and editor with the magazine *Monopol* in Berlin. She studied visual communication in Würzburg and for the last twelve years has been writing about art, design, and fashion for specialist and general publications including *form* and the *Frankfurter Rundschau.*

Markus Zehentbauer is a freelance journalist and editor based in Munich. He writes about art and design for the *Süddeutsche Zeitung* newspaper and the magazine *form.* Zehentbauer studied art history in Munich, worked at the Museum of Concrete Art in Ingolstadt, and was chief staff writer of *form* in Basel.

Photo Credits

Sabine Ahlbrand-Dornseif, Münster 285 (fig. 2)
Sophie Aigner/arturimages 281 (fig. 2)
Grégoire Alexandre 194
Daici Ano 210
M. Aukes 188, 216
Iwan Baan 71
Anders Sune Berg 21
janbitter.de 255, 260, 281 (figs. 1, 3), 282 (figs. 5, 6)
Paola Bobba 125
Thomas Brown 42, 101, 159
Cappellini 301 (fig. 2)
Studio Claerbout 133
ClassiCon 211, 289 (figs. 1, 5), 290 (fig. 9)
Cécile Clos, Nantes 77
Pelle Crepin 19
croce & wir fotostudio 30, 31
Marc Domage 305 (fig. 1), 306 (fig. 7)
Charles Duprat 34, 110
Peter Eder 22
edra 123, 277–278 (all figs.)
Marc Eggimann 163, 301 (fig. 4)
Carsten Eisfeld 150
Ivo Faber 55, 228, 273
Marina Faust 76, 198, 212, 252
David Franck, Ostfildern 15, 224, 225
Front 94, 185, 204
Mario Gastinger photographics, Munich 26, 202, 222
Giovanni Giannoni 66, 189
Fabrice Gousset 97, 98 132, 145, 203
Tomaz Gregoric 262
Studio Katharina Grosse 48
Steffen Groß 153
Roland Halbe Fotografie, Stuttgart 99, 108, 114, 238, 264
Rob 't Hart 127
Hayonstudio 85, 112, 152, 190, 214
Jochen Helle/arturimages 254, 282 (fig. 4)
Florian Holzherr 192
Maarten van Houten 18, 116, 191
Eduard Hueber/archphoto 117
Nick Kane 47
Kartell 23
Gerhard Kassner, Berlin 239
Yong-Kwan Kim 160, 161
kleinefenn@ifrance.com 118, 147
Matthias Kolb 88, 151, 199, 270, 141, 305 (figs. 2, 3), 306 (figs. 4–6)
Harold Koopmans 215
Robert Kot, Brussels 41, 170, 246
Ingmar Kurth 60, 218, 232, 263
Morgane Le Gall 302 (fig. 7)
Jonas Lencer 53
Åke E:son Lindman 44, 90, 144
Ricardo Loureiro 269
Moreno Maggi 155
Duccio Malagamba 166
Attilio Maranzano 58
Andreas Meichsner, Berlin 40
Dave Morgan 33, 156
Museen der Stadt Landshut, Harry Zdera 286 (fig. 5)
MVRDV 126
Myrzik & Jarisch 80
Jaime Navarro 68, 69
Monika Nikolic/arturimages 103
Mark O'Flaherty 136, 168
Takumi Ota 177, 201
Paul Ott 135
Alistair Overbruck 111, 251, 253
Alessandro Paderni 213, 290 (fig. 7)
Andreas Pauly 28, 86, 120, 285 (fig. 1)
Inga Powilleit 109, 236
Ed Reeve 267
Rheinisches Bildarchiv, Cologne 257
Christian Richters/arturimages 54, 293 (figs. 1, 3), 294 (figs. 4, 6, 7)
Paúl Rivera/archphoto.com 36, 73
Philippe Ruault 56, 57
Niels Schabrod 137
Johannes Schwartz 230
Florian Seidel, Munich 285 (fig. 3), 286 (fig. 6)
Jan Siefke, Shanghai 113
Timothy Soar 20
Oliver Spies 209
Städtische Galerie im Lenbachhaus, Munich, (Simone Gänsheimer) 286 (fig. 4)
Paul Tahon 302 (fig. 6)
Paul Tahon and Ronan & Erwan Bouroullec 67, 84, 301 (figs. 1, 3), 302 (figs. 5, 8)
Martin Url 226, 271
Hans-Jörg Walter 129, 165, 195, 217
Uwe Walter 171, 181
Ellen Page Wilson 72
Astrid Zuidema 139

Editing: Barbara Glasner, Berit Liedtke, Petra Schmidt, Markus Zehentbauer

Book idea: Barbara Glasner

Interviews and texts: Jens Asthoff, Markus Frenzl, Oliver Herwig, Silke Hohmann, Markus Zehentbauer

Translation from German into English: Adam Blauhut and Joseph O'Donnell

Copy editing: Julia Dawson

Layout, cover design and typography: Surface Gesellschaft für Gestaltung mbH, Frankfurt; Pascal Kress, Katrin Tüffers, Markus Weisbeck

Library of Congress Control Number: 2009934982

Bibliographic information published by the German National Library
The German National Library lists this publication in the Deutsche Nationalbibliografie; detailed bibliographic data are available on the Internet at http://dnb.d-nb.de.

This book is also available in a German language edition
(ISBN 978-3-0346-0091-0).

Basel · Boston · Berlin
P.O. Box 133, CH-4010 Basel, Switzerland
Part of Springer Science+Business Media

Lithography: Lithotronic Media GmbH, Dreieich

Printed on acid-free paper produced from chlorine-free pulp. TCF ∞

Printed in Germany

ISBN 978-3-0346-0092-7

9 8 7 6 5 4 3 2 1
www.birkhauser.ch